① 28/2/83

80p

POLITICS
thro' the Looking Glass

Stan Windass

POLITICS

THRO' THE
LOOKING GLASS

Stan Windass

NEW FOUNDATIONS

NEW FOUNDATIONS
The Rookery, Adderbury, Banbury OX17 3NA

First Published 1981
© Stan Windass 1981

ISBN 0 907650 00 7

Cover design: Shirley Edwards
Illustrations: Micheline Mason
Typesetting by: Rural Planning Services, Didcot
Printed in England by: Cox & Wyman Ltd., Reading
Production Consultant: Bill Cracknell

CONTENTS

Chapter Seven

ENERGY: THE PROBLEMS

Chapter Eight

ENERGY: BUILDING THE BRIDGE

Chapter Nine

THE INTERNATIONAL DIMENSION: DEFENCE

Chapter Ten

DEFENCE: CHANGING THE MEANING

Chapter Eleven

THE SHAPE OF GOVERNMENT

Appendix

INTRODUCTION
by
Shirley Williams

What government is for is not a question many of us
ask. Government is a fact, dominating, inescapable
and demanding. In a democracy, it is supposed to be
the servant of the people, accountable to them and
only trespassing upon their lives when the lives,
property or well-being of others are threatened. Yet
in practice it has become a regulator, a mentor, and a
provider. It seeks to perpetuate every function it
acquires. Like the corpse in Ionescu's play *Amedée,*
it fills whatever spaces remain uncluttered by law and
regulation.

Yet it is necessary to remember why democratic
governments increased in size and capacity in the last
three decades. They did so to compensate for the
inequalities created by private concentrations of
power which failed to provide a reasonable quality of
life for the majority of citizens. To argue that the
best government is the least government is to deny
the obvious improvements in the health, educational
opportunities and welfare enjoyed by the generations
born since the Second World War.

Standing aside from this well-worn argument about
more government or less, Stan Windass dares to ask
what government is for, and concludes that it is for
the maintenance and promotion of human rights. He

ix

interprets this in terms of the individual, not, as a Marxist would, in terms of the collective society. Human rights are about the individual's right to life, to work, to a home, to adequate means of livelihood, to a share in shaping government itself. He recognises the paradox that if government seeks to provide all the things human beings have a right to, it may destroy individuality itself. The central question he asks about jobs, for instance, is not how the government can employ all the people, but how can the government enable people to create work?

The idea of government as enabling — neither universal provider nor negative referee — is a creative and largely unexplored one. The enabling government would tackle unemployment by creating a better atmosphere for new enterprise, small business and innovation, and by establishing a network of opportunities for training and retraining. It would encourage a wide variety of jobs of different shapes and sizes — shared jobs, short-time jobs, intermittent jobs, jobs that change their character. In housing, the enabling government would not prevent people buying or improving their council houses. It would deal with housing shortages by making working capital and finance available for those who wanted to build their own houses, or to convert and adapt existing housing. It would stimulate a spectrum of forms of ownership and of tenancy, such as shared ownership, part rent-part mortgage, cooperatives and housing associations. It would break down the segregation of housing which is so crucial a factor in sustaining Britain's class system.

An enabling government will always weigh its actions against the undesirability of doing anything that might diminish the sum total of human freedom and self-determination. "Freedom and self-determination are the 'sea' out of which the stronger rights emerge" says Stan Windass. These stronger rights resemble amphibious creatures, in being dependent

x

upon the sea of freedom for their conception and survival. So government must draw back, must leave a space for individuals to flourish in and to develop. In many ways it is a Lockeian idea, an unwritten social contract between individual human beings and government, yet an idea brought up to date by the recognition that many forces in modern society impinge upon individual freedom, such as environmental pollution or powerful corporations or mass communications, and therefore need to be controlled, and can only be controlled by government itself.

In addition to its prime function of enabling its citizens to realise their rights and freedoms, a function that may, but need not, involve providing and purchasing goods and services, Stan Windass sees government as a trustee of society's resources, above all such non-renewable resources as land, minerals and fossil fuels. Energy, he argues, should be regarded not as wealth — the planet's finite supplies of fossil fuel — but as income, from the sun, wind, water and biomass. The world must then live within its income, and can indeed do so by a proper regulation of its own demand. He illustrates our strange short-term sense of priorities by pointing to the way in which materials, including energy, are often subsidised or sold cheaply, while labour is taxed and made more expensive.

His is an attractive vision, and one worked out in detail in employment policy, housing, energy and defence to show how it might work in practice. I have only two reservations, but they are large ones. The first is how to deal with those rights and powers established by interest-groups which make it difficult or even impossible to enable the whole body of citizens to enjoy freedom of choice or initiative. Alternative schools and health systems run into strong resistance from professional organisations. Self-builders and house repairers are suspect to trade unions and direct labour organisations. These organised interests have been essential to the winning of high

xi

professional standards and to the establishment of workers' rights. But they now impinge as much upon individual human rights as does any government of a democracy. What the individual in a democracy can do is at least in part determined today by big business, big trade unions and professional bodies. The Universal Declaration of Human Rights hardly recognises their existence. The dilemma is a grave one. How can the government enable individuals to enjoy greater freedom if its own power is less than that of the interest group? How can it decentralise and devolve power unless they do the same? The issue is rarely tackled, yet it seems to me that the powers of government can only be devolved if the powers of these over-mighty subjects are devolved too, for example by anti-trust laws compelling the break-up of monopolies, or by the free election of worker representatives at plant and workshop level. Nothing illustrates better what happens when governments are weaker than the interest groups within them than the plight of the so-called 'banana republics' of Central and Latin America, dominated by a handful of foreign-owned companies.

The second reservation concerns the characteristics of human beings themselves. Those who fight for their own rights rarely recognise the rights of others. Many a bold revolutionary on whose banner is inscribed the word 'freedom', treats his wife, girlfriend or daughter with contempt. The plight of women in much of the independent Third World does not bear thinking about. Elsewhere, self-governing majorities oppress racial or cultural minorities. The whole disagreeable subject of conflicting rights is too easily subsumed in the shouts of the triumphant victors.

These reservations do not subtract from the freshness and relevance of what Stan Windass has to say. A new radical movement is sending up small shoots in Britain now. This book makes an important contribution to that movement, vital, imaginative and humane.

AUTHOR'S PREFACE

The purpose of this book is to look at politics 'through the looking-glass' of human rights, and to see if this helps us to understand what is right and what is wrong about the present system.

Because of the growth of government and the mystification which surrounds it, many of us now feel confused about what government is really for. We tend to gang up in ideologies of the right or the left, and to demand more government action or less, without giving sufficient thought to what kind of things government does well, and what kind of things it does badly.

We take for granted for instance that government alone can provide all kinds of necessary goods and services — like the police and fire services, refuse collection, and homes for the down-and-out. Yet this is not necessarily true. In the U.S.A. there are now many private fire services, which, having discovered that three-quarters of all calls are for small fires in litter bins, cars or gardens, now provide small 'attack trucks' manned by two people at one tenth the cost of a full engine. New Jersey has a private police force. Southend has contracted out its refuse collection; and Tony Williamson, the star of the television series 'Down and out in London', found that after horrifying experiences of public and voluntary sector 'hostels' for the poor, he was eventually best and most respectfully accommodated at a cost he could afford in a hostel run as a business company!

This certainly does *not* mean that what we need is just less government. The argument of this book is that we need strong government — but a government that has clear objectives. These objectives should be above all to maintain and promote human rights. But promoting human rights does not mean providing an ever-lengthening list of goods and services. The social body like the physical body, is well able to cope with its own needs.

The purpose of government is to draw up 'rules of the game' which ensure that society functions in a context of justice, and to release the latent creative energies of the people. All human rights are rooted in freedom and self-determination.

If a government systematically neglects its duty and oppresses the people, then in one way or another the people will eventually rise up in protest and destroy such a government — and perhaps much else besides. This is the lesson of liberation movements from Czarist Russia to Poland, and from ancient Israel to El Salvador; but it has echoes close to home in our own apparently secure democracies. The ever-growing force of a people claiming freedom and dignity is at once the greatest peril and the greatest hope for mankind. It is for those of us who believe in democracy to harness these powerful forces of the human spirit to creative rather than to destructive ends.

The human rights approach has to be both tough and flexible. Human rights are not just a set of rules written down in declarations and international covenants — though the fact that they are written down is important. There is a growing and world-wide consensus that all human beings have certain basic needs, that all are equally entitled to respect, and that this respect must be incorporated in rights.

The gradual clarification of these rights is the very essence of politics and is the only path that leads towards a world order based on justice.

ACKNOWLEDGEMENTS

The author wishes to thank the following who helped him to make sense of the following pages:

Anthony de Reuck	Elaine Sexton
Brian Duckworth	Graeme Shankland
Jean Hollis	Nicholas Simms
Keith Jackson	Peter Stead
George McRobie	Dick Taverne
James Robertson	Lorna Windass

He also wishes to thank Michael Boddington without whose support the book could not have been published.

Chapter One
WHAT SHOULD GOVERNMENT BE ABOUT?

Many people have a love/hate relationship with government. On the one hand they are secretly proud of the democratic traditions it embodies, and believe that if only the right party gets in it will lead us all towards a utopia of plenty and justice; but on the other hand they see it as an oppressive system presided over by squabbling politicians and dominated by inscrutable civil servants.

Part of the difficulty is that we are confused about the purpose of government. The first two chapters seek to throw light on this matter.

THE MEANING OF GOVERNMENT

To 'govern' means to make rules and regulations to control the behaviour of groups of people, and to have some kind of authority to ensure that these rules and regulations are carried out.

In this sense we have all kinds of 'governments', ranging from the local darts club committee to the United Nations. They all have power to regulate certain aspects of our lives, and some authority to see that the regulations are carried out. Government is a commonplace feature of social life, and it appears in a thousand different shapes and sizes.

1

In our country the first experience a child has of government is normally in the family, where the parents have a very wide-ranging legal and moral authority over the growing child, matched by duties of care and education owed to the child.

As the child grows up, he becomes involved in other communities or groups, such as the school community and the work community, all of which have their own system of government, which he is obliged to accept if he wants to be part of the group.

However this is not what most of us mean by 'The Government'. Amongst all these groups which organise our behaviour the growing person becomes more and more aware of an over-arching 'Government' which seems to be quite unlike all the others. It is remote, and all-embracing. It is backed up by folk-lore, and associated in our minds with kings and queens, battles and pageantry. In spite of its remoteness, it somehow seems to be part of ourselves. The impression we have is that its powers are not limited to any particular field — like chess or education — and that it can make rules about anything and everything. Its only limitation is territorial; it appears to hold supreme power in a particular plot of land. We normally have no choice as to whether we join the group which accepts the authority of the government, because we are born 'under' it, and it is not usual to think of leaving it.

In reality of course the government cannot do anything it chooses. It is constrained by the unwritten 'constitutional law', and increasingly constrained by other power groups within society — like multinational companies or the trade unions. All the same there is an important element of truth in the child's perception of the over-arching authority. Since the nineteenth century most legal theorists have accepted Austin's view that parliament enjoys unrestricted legislative 'sovereignty' — that it can in principle make any rules it likes, and command absolute obedience. At the same time, as government has increasingly taken on the job of provider and manager, it has tended to become the natural focus or 'super-committee' where all problems must ultimately be resolved.

We have now reached a stage in the development of human society when we have to grow out of this rather infantile attitude. We have to ask the crude question, 'What is Government really for?' — and we have to go on asking it until we reach a satisfactory answer. We now have to ask whether it makes any real sense that we should elect a super-committee at Westminster (or Brussels) to do anything they choose or to represent us about everything. We do not normally elect committees of people to do anything they choose. We do not normally appoint representatives to represent us about everything.

The idea of sovereignty has both a long history and deep roots in the human psyche. It has its psychological origins in the family and tribal structure and the commonly felt need for a father-figure, a totem or a supernatural being to whom we owe our identity, safety, and allegiance. The mediaeval belief in a personal God who managed the universe was reflected in political systems, merging with the Roman tradition of the divine emperor; Kings and Queens rule as God's appointed agents. As the idea of God's absolute sovereignty faded, monarchs and eventually sovereign states claimed power without restriction.

Democracy, an idea which began its history in the small Greek city states, is at the opposite pole from this tradition. Whereas sovereignty originates in an absolute claim by someone to have a divine right to lord it over anyone else, the basic idea of democracy is that no-one has a god-given right to govern or dominate another, but that the source of power is in the people, the 'demos'.

At some stage in the eighteenth century however, a kind of nuclear fusion of ideas occurred between democracy and sovereignty. The people took over the

3

nation state — and at the same time, the nation state took over the people. Political thinkers and philosophers started talking about the 'sovereign will' of the people as a whole. The idea was accepted that the state in some magical way actually *was* the people (or should be); and there could be no 'us and them', because all was one; and the sovereign will of 'the people', expressed in the state, was absolute — just like the pretentious claim of the old kings and queens. The sovereign will of the people in a perfect democracy just *had* to be right — there was nothing else to judge it by. The Democratic State became a kind of God.

Subsequently the philosopher Hegel declared that

> Truth is the unity of the universal and subjective Will, and the universal is to be found in the State, in its laws, its universal and rational arrangements. The State is the Divine Idea as it exists on earth.

THE NEED TO RE-THINK

There is therefore a considerable baggage of ideas and prejudices which stand in our way when we try to think straight about what government is for; the time has now come when we must make the effort. There are a number of reasons why this is so.

First of all there is the problem of the 'cancer-state' which creeps into every aspect of our lives. The term 'cancer-state' is not used here abusively, but in the precise sense of growth without definition and control, the kind of morbid cell-multiplication which leads to the death of the human organism.

The characteristic of the present time is the enormous size and power of government machinery, compared with the position even twenty years ago. Local Government employs directly two million people, and the Central Government nearly one million people. This is about one sixth of the total available workforce in the country, and includes civil servants, the educational establishment, the public services (like transport

4

and electricity), the medical establishment, the police, the armed forces, and a very large workforce concerned with local authority housing and public buildings. The number of people directly employed by the state has probably increased ten-fold in the last generation; in the past century it has increased one hundred-fold.

The volume of legislation is also immense compared with the recent past. It is estimated now that 2000 pages of new legislation are processed by Parliament every year, and very little is repealed. The volume of legislation has been increasing for some time in an exponential curve.

This growth of state activities has been accepted partly because of the psychological and historical pre-conditioning that we have described, and partly because of genuine aspirations to social justice. It is sometimes argued by those concerned with social justice that a fair distribution of essential goods and services can only be achieved by a centralised sharing-out process. It is also argued that this central process must be carried out by representatives of the people who are publicly accountable, and that accountability is guaranteed through the democratic state.

The aspiration towards justice is a worthy one, and the arguments are serious. They are arguments however that lead in the direction of ever increasing governmental functions, and which therefore eventually will force us either to hack away indiscriminately at the 'cancer' — or, more wisely, to go to the root of the problem, define the objectives of government and establish limits to government power.

Refusal to face the problem of ever increasing government, whether through doctrinaire conviction or through idleness, leads in the direction of totalitarianism. In the totalitarian state general objectives (often worthy ones) are pursued without regard for human rights and eventually this must imply control of the media, elimination of organised opposition, and

5

extensive use of internal enforcement procedures. The challenge of totalitarianism in our present society comes both from the right and from the left of the political spectrum.

There are two other reasons why it is essential at this point in history to rethink the basis of government.

One is the problem of overlapping government, or overlapping spheres of jurisdiction. The European Communities Act of 1972 acknowledges the existence of a source of law and of a court uncontrolled by our parliament, and as we know this law has already had wide repercussions in this country. Whatever attitude we take to the Common Market, the problem of overlapping jurisdiction is one which is bound to increase as the world community becomes more complex and more interrelated. Tasks we associate commonly with government increasingly have to be carried out at levels other than that of the nation state. It is impossible to go on thinking therefore that there is in any territory just one centre of government. The common sense approach to such a problem is to say that governmental tasks should be carried out on whatever scale is necessary or functionally appropriate — but, if there is a choice, on the smallest scale possible. Regulations about international telecommunications are best made on a world-wide scale; and regulations about footpaths by the Parish Council.

This means that instead of monolithic government, with all the trappings of power and claims of absolute allegiance, we should have lots of overlapping and interlocking systems of rule-making with different centres and different spheres of jurisdiction. The symbolic mystique of state sovereignty must then begin to crumble; no longer able to rest on the assumption that government is 'for everything', we shall then be forced to make discriminating judgements.

The second reason is the growing international movement for human rights, which can be seen negatively as an unescapable challenge to former notions of national sovereignty, and positively as the foundation of a new international order, a new focus of political action, and a new definition of legitimate government. It is this movement above all which obliges us now to question the basis of political power.

GOVERNMENT AND HUMAN RIGHTS

How then can we answer the question, 'What is Government for?' I believe there is a simple response to this simple question which now merits serious attention. It is that Government exists for the purpose of promoting and maintaining human rights; and that its power to make laws or rules is both defined and limited by this purpose.

There would have been nothing surprising about such a definition of the Government role before the advent of the modern nation state. The basic human rights are life and liberty; the kingdoms have always stood as the alleged protectors of the people, defending them against enemies both within and without, and maintaining the 'king's peace'. The feudal system offered a precise formulation of the typical bargain; the warrior chief will protect you, and leave you in peace, provided you help him to do so by contributing to his maintenance and doing a share of military service. Although not formulated in terms of human rights, the bargain was a clear one and the system relatively stable.

Government is much more complicated nowadays (though it could be argued that the same simple bargain could be there in relation to defence), and it might seem presumptuous to put forward such a simplistic idea as the concept of human rights as being both the touchstone of good government and the test of its legitimacy. Indeed, fifty years ago the idea would have been considered untenable in practice. 'What are human rights?' would have been the scornful question. 'Are these part of the natural law? Which natural law? On which tablet of stone was it written down?'

The situation today however is rather different. First of all there are some very clear answers to the question 'What are human rights?' in documents formally ratified by most governments in the world, and these answers are astonishingly far-reaching. They are the outcome of a long period of gradual crystallisation of people's profound beliefs and aspirations into codified laws with world-wide implications. Secondly, there is a powerful world-wide movement seeking to make political sense of the concept of fundamental human rights.

The idea that government has no other purpose than to maintain and promote human rights is by no means new. It was stated in a straightforward way by Tom Paine in the eighteenth century, in his famous book *The Rights of Man*. Quoting from the second article in the French Declaration of the Rights of Man and of the Citizen (which he helped to compile), he wrote,

> The end of all political association is the preservation of the natural and imprescriptable rights of man. These rights are liberty, property, security, and the right to resist oppression.

Associated with this view of political activity was his equally down-to-earth view of government as a 'manager', delegated by the people to look after certain communal affairs, and deriving its authority necessarily from the 'nation', which thereafter always retained the right to give it the sack.

The government's task of maintaining and promoting human rights includes derived duties which deserve special attention. One is the duty of the government to maintain order in the most general sense of a coherent system of rules. People have a right to an orderly social system. Whatever the purpose of rules, they must mesh together to enable society to function in a predictable way. Some

8

rules have no other justification than the principle of order — like driving on the left hand side of the road, for instance, In other cases there is confusion arising from conflicting rules — like those connected with the Social Security system for instance — and it is important to clarify the system simply on the grounds of good order. A reasonably stable money system also is essential for the country and for the world on the grounds of order, apart from other human rights considerations.

The second derived duty is that of trusteeship. Government must exercise a function as community trustee over certain basic resources such as the land, the air and the sea. Pollution of the environment directly affects the communal rights which society as a whole must possess in the air we breathe, the sun which shines on us, and the water we drink. There must be a body which expresses and safeguards such rights, and for this also the model of trusteeship is appropriate.

Of even more importance however is the rights of future generations. Only the living have votes. Few people would deny however that we carry a responsibility for the future; and many would see this responsibility stretching forward through countless generations. To give expression to this responsibility, in a finite world of non-renewable resources, we must act as trustees for future generations, and the government has both the right and the duty to exercise control over resources to fulfil this trust.

WHAT ARE RIGHTS? — The Presumption of Freedom

We presume, in any normal human society, that people have a right to do what they are doing, unless there is proof to the contrary. This proof has to be based on the fact that they are infringing someone else's right, or neglecting an obligation which is related to someone else's right. So there is a general sense of the word 'right' in which we have a right to do anything at all which does not infringe someone else's stronger right.

9

It is in fact impossible to visualise a human society in which such a presumption of freedom does not hold, although in regimes which depend on might rather than right this basic presumption is challenged by arbitrary arrest, direction, detention, or even execution. Although this can be called a weak and general sense of the word right, it is an important foundation for all thinking about human rights in a stronger sense. Human rights in the weak and general sense include 'rights' to do all manner of things, many of them of no consequence and many of which we would personally disapprove. People in general have a right to swear at each other — though not to threaten each other with violence. People have a right to stay in bed all day — and for that matter to walk around the streets all night (although the police don't always seem to approve!); and it is now proposed, very sensibly, to remove drunkeness from the list of crimes so that people will have a right to be drunk (though not to be drunk and *disorderly*, which could be said to involve other people's rights in a strong sense).

As with all rights, there is a corresponding implied duty. If someone has a right to do something, other people have a corresponding duty. In the case of the rights in the general and weak sense, the corresponding duty is equally general and equally weak. The duty corresponding to the general right of freedom is the duty not to interfere coercively. If the proposed change in the law of drunkeness goes through, then we shall all (including the police) have a duty *not* to interfere coercively with those exercising their right to be drunk — just as we have a duty not to interfere coercively with anyone going about his or her normal business.

Rights in the Stronger Sense

What then are the rights in the stronger sense, which can go beyond, and perhaps cut across the presumption of freedom?

10

In general, all the stronger and more specific rights give the bearer of the right some kind of claim on others, imposing on them a duty, whether individually or collectively, to facilitate, promote, maintain or guarantee this right. No-one would make such a claim for the right to be drunk, even if the law were changed; but we do legitimately make such a claim with regard to the right to education, to work, or to protection against murderers.

In practice, there is no fixed dividing-line between rights in the weak and general sense, and rights in the stronger sense. The balance between the two is continuously changing, the process is an historical and evolutionary one, the result of struggle and debate and political action rather than of logical analysis. There is however an important difference, and there always will be, between rights in the weak and general sense and rights in the stronger sense, and we must not be confused by the changing borderline. To draw an analogy, the borderline between the sea and land is also continuously changing; but the sea remains forever quite distinct from the land.

The 'sea' of rights in the weak sense is the general context of freedom within which we normally operate; the 'land' consists of our stronger and specific rights which are by general consensus considered necessary for human fulfilment. The land and sea together form the landscape; the land emerges from the sea, and the sea gives shape to the land. Without the context of freedom, stronger rights have no meaning. The right to work cannot mean the right to be told what to do, and the right to a home cannot mean the right to be put in a box with a roof.

The content of the human rights consensus, and along with it the meaning of fulfilment, will vary from time to time and from place to place; but this does not mean that the definition is arbitrary, or that we cannot distinguish a direction of progress. The world-wide history of the human rights movement shows a high degree of convergence.

11

Human rights in the stronger and specific sense are generated through the process of custom, legislation and political action. We can all participate in this process; but first we must understand how it works. It is important to begin where we are, and not in abstractions. An important aspect of 'where we are' is to be found in the established sources of international law, in the form of treaties and international covenants. Anyone not familiar with the scope of this 'statute law' of human rights in this sense will be staggered by its extent. In relation to Employment, for instance, not only is the right incorporated in international covenants, but has been formally accepted in declarations of policy by numerous states of every variety of economic structure and outlook. We also need to look to 'customary law'. Just as in a family solemn declarations of principle and practice gradually build up into a 'customary law' which it is increasingly difficult to contradict, so these formal declarations about rights help to constitute a 'customary law' of mankind. Out of such a background of consensus, various forms of pressure for compliance are bound to emerge.

We must not however limit our view of human rights to what is laid down in legal documents and declarations. These documents, though important, are themselves a manifestation of thought and aspiration, often very untidy at the edges, in which we all have to participate. It is part of the process of declaring where we all stand in relation to our fellow human beings. In this great movement, politics and law are intimately related. The law is a kind of deposited tradition which sets the ground rules; but politics must aspire beyond this. Politics is the factory of human rights.

The common tradition of legal theory today is 'positivist' — i.e. it says the law is just what exists in explicit rules, and that is that. But this does not help

12

us to decide what *should* exist as law. To decide that we have to look to a further 'source' of law, something like what was meant in the Middle Ages by 'natural law'. This does not mean that we imagine tablets of stone coming down from heaven; nor does it mean that we sit in our studies like seventeenth or eighteenth century philosophers and work out a purely rational clockwork theory depending on some highly abstract concept of an individual. It means simply that we must use our sense of natural justice. To get from where we are to somewhere a little further forward in terms of human rights, is to think about ourselves and the people we know, in all their untidy individuality, including people in quite different cultures from our own, and ask ourselves what seem to be the really basic common needs for fulfilment which are not already sufficiently explicit in human rights legislation. If we think wisely, our case will be heard. If we can then make our beliefs real in political action and commitment, we shall be working in the human rights factory producing tools of liberation.

We must however exercise caution in proposing new rights or new directions of advance.

There are two important reasons for this caution. The first is that if we are seeking wide consensus and political involvement, this must be based on a few simple concepts. The second is that there is an important sense in which, by indiscriminately extending the 'land' of rights in the stronger sense, we diminish the 'sea' of rights in the weak sense. For instance, we might decide as a community that we really do not like people swearing at each other, or being drunk, or walking around in the middle of the night, and we might say we and our children have a right to a social environment free from profanity, or drunkeness, or noise at night, and we might legislate to that effect. We would then establish appropriate control systems and policy, and we would make considerable inroads into the sea of general rights on which we all depend for our well-being.

13

The same argument applies to more serious matters. There is a way of defining and enlarging the right to a home, for instance by excessive tenant protection, such that people with houses are severely limited in their general right to do what they wish with these houses — such as to accommodate a temporary tenant. It would be an even more severe invasion of the sea of general rights if compulsory billeting were used as a means of guaranteeing the right to a home (though this is necessary in extreme circumstances). Similarly, there is a way of defining and promoting the right to work which invades the freedom to enter into mutually agreed work contracts.

In either case, in housing or work, it can be shown that certain legislation designed to promote certain human rights can have the effect of damaging those rights. The social body, like the human body, has its own self-curing systems; these often require external aid, but preferably by an approach which stimulates the body's own self-curing system, rather than one which overrides the body's mechanisms with alien forces.

Rights and Duties

It is of the greatest importance to understand that rights and duties are correlative ideas — it is quite impossible to separate one from the other. There is a tendency when people talk about rights to assume they are talking about *claiming* rights. But for every right there are two groups of people — those who can justly claim it and those who have a duty to respect it. The rights of the child are the duties of parents; and the rights of parents are the duties of the child.

The government has a duty to construct a society in which human rights are maintained; and this duty implies a right to make appropriate rules and a duty on the part of the people to obey. To talk about a human rights government is therefore not the same as talking about the 'entitlement society', it is rather

14

to stress the binding nature of the contract which holds us together in a human society.

THE HISTORICAL TRADITION – *Roots*

There are several historical roots to the present human rights legislation. One is the tradition of rules for regulating the conduct of warfare, improving the lot of prisoners of war and of the wounded, protecting non-combatants and outlawing the use of weapons of mass-destruction. These rules are incorporated in the Hague and Geneva Conventions. Another is the work of the International Labour Organisation (ILO), which has been responsible for codifying the right to work.

Another root, going much deeper into history, is the tradition of equality before the law, and of the right to fair trial and the presumption of innocence, which is embedded in the Common Law and is now also part of the world-wide law of human rights.

The main tap-root of human rights thinking however is much more central to our civilisation and to the Christian doctrine of the brotherhood of man on which it is founded. This tradition is based on the idea of the equality and brotherhood of all men as children of God. It has gradually come to the surface in a whole series of declarations and codifications, best known of which are the famous proclamation of the 'Droits de l'homme' at the time of the French Revolution, and the American Declaration of Independence following closely afterwards, which asserted that:

> All men are created equal; they are endowed by their creator with certain inalienable rights; that among these are life, liberty and the pursuit of happiness; to secure these rights governments are instituted among men deriving their just powers from the consent of the government; that whenever any form of government becomes destructive of these ends it is the right of the people to alter or abolish it.

15

Throughout all the vagaries of history, a steady line of development links this Declaration to the major breakthrough achieved by the world community in the Universal Declaration of Human Rights, proclaimed by the U.N. General Assembly on December 10, 1948 (Human Rights Day) without a dissenting vote (for full text, see appendix).

The Declaration (though not in itself legally binding on states), was the seed-bed of a new world order. Most of the declaration is part of the 'customary law' of nations. A major part has been written into the constitutions of 30 new states; and the Universal Declaration itself became the source of numerous protocols and covenants which are legally binding on signatory states. Outstanding among these are the Covenant on Civil and Political Rights, and the Covenant on Economic, Social and Cultural Rights, both of which came into force following 35 ratifications for each in 1976.

Meanwhile a European Convention for the Protection of Human Rights and Fundamental Freedoms has been adopted by the members of the Council of Europe and is now in force. This convention is itself an attempt by countries with a common heritage of political conditions, ideals, freedom and the rule of law to take the first steps for the collective enforcement of certain of the rights stated in the Universal Declaration. It deals only with civil liberties but defines them with considerably more precision than the Universal Declaration; it establishes a European Commission of Human Rights competent to examine petitions from individuals concerning violations of the convention by governments which have accepted the competence of the Commission, and a European Court of Human Rights competent to deal with cases referred to it by a contracting party or by the Commission.

16

The First and Second Articles of the Universal
Declaration of Human Rights read as follows:

> All Human beings are born free and equal in dignity and
> rights. They are endowed with reason and conscience and
> should act towards one another in a spirit of brother-
> hood. Everyone is entitled to all the rights and freedoms
> set forth in this Declaration, without distinction of any
> kind, such as race, colour, sex, language, religion, politi-
> cal or other opinion, national or social origin, property,
> birth or status. Furthermore, no distinction shall be made
> on the basis of the political, jurisdictional or international
> status of the country or territory to which a person
> belongs, whether it be independent, trust, non-self-
> governing or under any other limitation of sovereignty.

The statement that 'all human beings are born free
and equal in dignity and rights' can easily be assailed
philosophically as neither self-evidently true, nor even
comprehensible. Yet it is the foundation of all that
follows. It is basically an *option* — a stance we take
up, not at random, but because at a level deeper than
that of rationality we sense that it is right. If anyone
rejects or ridicules this stance, the dispute cannot be
resolved by rational debate alone.

It is astonishing that this statement is enshrined as
a universal principle in a document which has received
the formal assent of representatives of virtually the
entire population of the world. The principle implies
decisive rejection of totalitarianism, which confers on
collectives or specific groups rights of control and
domination over others. Social and political systems
have been built and are still built on this contrary
assumption, sometimes explicit and sometimes
implicit. It may be that in the long-term perspective
mankind is at a point where the basic option has to be
taken up once and for all and it is an option which
cuts right across traditional political alignments of
right and left.

The first cluster of rights following from these basic

declarations of faith are related to the right to life and to freedom.* They include, for example, the closest approximation that can be made at this time to a prohibition of the death penalty, as a direct consequence of the fundamental right to life.

A second cluster of rights relates to freedom of expression and the right to participate in public affairs.† This includes the rights of peaceful assembly, freedom of association, and freedom of religious belief and practice.

Other articles of the Declaration and Covenants are connected with the right to work.** These include the right of access to suitable training programmes adapted to work opportunities, the right to just remuneration, to satisfactory work conditions, and to a choice of work.

The right to an adequate standard of living, to a healthy environment and access to health care are also affirmed.†† The articles safeguarding this right make it clear that there is an obligation on all parties to the Covenant to co-operate internationally to achieve a just distribution of world food supplies in relation to need.

Other Articles of the Declaration and Covenant proclaim the right to education directed to the 'full development of the human personality', to freedom of movement (including protection against deportation), to ownership of personal property, and to the protection of the family as 'the natural and fundamental group unit of society.'

* Articles 3-12 and 14-16 of the *International Declaration of Human Rights* and 6-11 of the *International Covenant on Civil and Political Rights.*
† Articles 18-22 of the *International Covenant on Civil and Political Rights* and 18-21 of the *International Declaration.*
** Articles 6-8 of the *International Covenant on Economic, Social and Cultural Rights*, and 23-24 of the *International Declaration.*
†† Articles 11 and 12 of the *International Covenant on Economic, Social and Cultural Rights* and 25 of the *International Declaration.*

These rights which are proclaimed in the Universal Declaration have been divided into two categories in subsequent documents: *Economic and Social* rights like work, food and education, are distinguished from *Civil and Political* rights which are to do with freedom and political organisation. On the whole, the western nations use the term human rights to refer to Civil and Political Rights, and the communist countries use the term to refer to economic rights. Western nations therefore tend to use the term human rights as a stick to beat communists, pointing to abuse of freedom in communist countries, and the communist countries use their version of human rights as a stick to beat the capitalist nations, pointing to unemployment, bad housing and poverty.

Clearly there is no future in limiting the term human rights to one or the other side in this debate. Both sides are resoundingly and undeniably right, and each side can legitimately base its case on documents solemnly ratified by both. Economic Rights cannot possibly be separated from Civil and Political Rights. A vote is no use to a starving man; but a feast in prison is no answer to political persecution.

Of course there is a big difference between rights that can be enforced in courts of law and rights which must be fought for through political process. It is possible for a citizen of the U.K. to petition the European Commission of Human Rights about ill-treatment of prisoners (which is covered in the European Convention on Human Rights), but not about the right to work (which is covered by the European Social Charter).

This difference is however no reason for confining the use of the term 'human rights' either to the legally enforcible rights or to the non-legally enforcible rights; to do so would be to take sides in a sterile debate, and to emasculate the tradition which has been handed down to us through history.

19

Finally we must add to the set of Human Rights which have been internationally proclaimed a unique and special right with a fascinating history of its own and which underlies the entire structure of human rights — the Right of Self-Determination of People.* The principle of self-determination is written into the 2nd Article of the U.N. Charter, and the right to self-determination is the foundation stone of both the Economic and Political Covenants. The right is unique in the sense that it is a right originally accorded to large groups rather than to individuals; and yet its implications for individual rights are profound.

The principle of Self-Determination first emerged on the international scene in the war aims of the Allies in the First World War, when it was obviously in their interests to support the forces of nationalism which were disrupting the empires of their enemies the Turks and Austrians. It was never intended to apply to the empires of the allies themselves. However, such principles once proclaimed tend to have a life of their own, and can easily backfire against their operators. Churchill told parliament in 1941 that "he did not become the King's First Minister to preside over the liquidation of the British Empire", assuring them that the Charter principle of self-determination had no application outside Europe. Nevertheless he and subsequent British Prime Ministers did indeed preside over the dissolution of the Empire in accord with this very principle; and it has since acquired such status on the international stage that in spite of its vagueness no nation on earth can openly disregard it.

It is however a mistake to link self-determination too closely with nationalism and the break-up of empires, though this is how it originated. It could of course equally well apply to joining nations together

* For the working out of this right in practice, see *Frontier Disputes in International Relations*, ed. Evan Luard, chapter by Stan Windass, p. 22. (Thames & Hudson, 1970).

(the British entry into Europe, whether we like it or not, was decided in accord with the principle of self-determination); but the general implication of the principle of self-determination is even wider than this. It applies not only to the drawing-up of national boundaries, but to the choice of political system within those boundaries. It is the basis of the Citizens' right freely to choose their system of government, and to take part in political activity;* it implies that political authority is created by and depends on the free assent of individuals; and it appears as a recurring theme in the wording of other rights, such as the right to work (which must be freely chosen)†, and the right to education (according to parents wishes).**

The very 'unruliness' of the principle of freedom and self-determination is a sign of its vitality; and one way in which this unruliness shows itself is in the diversity of groups it can be said to apply to. There is a tendency for it to seep right down throughout society — to peoples, to minorities, to groups — and of course to individuals, because it is only our experience of individual choice that gives any meaning to larger concepts of group self-determination.

The way the argument works in practice is like this. A country subjugated by another can claim the right of self-determination to throw off its rulers; but it cannot then claim that self-determination gives it a right to dominate its own regions or minorities. Moreover, these regions and minorities may claim the right of self-determination but then they will need to justify in the same language their cultural attitudes to their own suppressed groups — such as women, for example. Ultimately the same principle must apply to the individual.

The principle of freedom and self-determination, as we have shown, has a life of its own — it cannot easily

* *Universal Declaration of Human Rights*, Article 21.
† Ibid Article 23.
** Ibid Article 26.

be confined. It is in fact the core-principle of the entire human rights movement. Freedom and self-determination is as it were the 'sea' out of which the stronger rights emerge, and which alone makes sense of these stronger rights. If we step back from the territory of codified law and think about what is happening in the field of liberation movements throughout society and throughout the world, we can see that the principle as a living force is one of the most pervasive influences on human history in our generation. Behind the storm-clouds of tyranny which threaten modern society, the sun of liberation is struggling to break through.

Chapter Two
CLARIFICATIONS

Human beings are essentially social creatures; in isolation they perish, and in society they flourish through elaborate and subtle forms of co-operation which have evolved with the use of language and symbolism. One way of looking at this social process is to see it as an exchange of goods and services. If the term 'goods and services' is interpreted widely enough, to include abstract values such as security or friendship, then this description of society as an exchange of goods and services can cover the whole communal life of a human group.

If the government's job is to make rules to ensure that human rights are maintained, and that order is preserved, how does it relate to this complex social process by which human society distributes and exchanges goods and services? First of all it is important to make some distinctions.

ENABLING AND PROVIDING

The first essential is to distinguish the general task of maintaining rights from the specific task of providing. There is a vast difference between these two ideas. We can easily see that the government may have a duty to guarantee the right to life; but it would seem odd to say that the government had a duty to *provide* life. Even the most extreme of totalitarian regimes would find that a strange statement. The fact is that human beings have for quite a long time been good at providing life — they simply have to be left to themselves (preferably with a reasonable amount of privacy). Perhaps in future generations 'providing work' will begin to sound as odd as providing life.

If freedom and self-determination is the core of human rights, and if human life is fundamentally about being rather than having, then increasingly we have to question the basic meaning of words like housing, health and education (all of which are without question human rights), and see them as aspects of what we are, rather than things we possess. They are all basically things we do, not things we get.

Of course there are cases where in order to maintain a basic right you have to provide. If a person is starving, you must provide him with food; if a person is living on the streets, he must be provided with shelter. Even in these extreme cases, however, there is a danger in just 'providing', as indicated in the proverb —

> Give a man a fish, and you feed him for a day; teach him to fish, and you feed him for a lifetime.

As our children grow up, we have to provide them with all kinds of things; but as wise parents, we know that all this providing from the very beginning is for the purpose of fostering self-determination, of forming an adult for whom we will no longer provide.

There is a particular danger for government in adopting the providing role as a basis for the realisation of human rights. Providing is tangible, it can be quantified, it can be programmed — just as at the baby clinic we can say how many grams of this and that and how many vitamin drops have been consumed. And governments have to justify themselves, have to be accountable, and therefore have to 'count'. Now there is undoubtedly an important providing role, as we have

24

said, for any government seriously concerned with justice and human rights; but because of the kind of institution which government is, there is a tendency for the very real concern with justice and human rights to be expressed more and more in 'providing' and 'counting' terms.

The dangers of this are profound. First of all, by identifying justice, equality, and human rights with countable objects, this kind of programme leads to a trivialisation of these basic concepts in everyone's mind, and this trivialisation leads to a drift towards the totalitarian providing state.

Secondly, by identifying the deepest human needs and aspirations (work, education, health, houses) with countable objects given out from the central source, the government is in danger of blocking the very well springs of human vitality and fulfilment. People begin to see themselves as objects defined as 'having' a set of things — house, television-set, car, etc. — all their basic so-called rights. To give people such a lifeless and soulless self-image is to destroy human rights as effectively as by gas chambers; and a population so schooled, since in reality it can never have its 'set of things', can only relate to the central distribution with apathy, indifference, or violence. Unfortunately the last option could be the only way out of the trap.

The opposite of providing is *'enabling'*. Enabling, properly defined, should be the basic mode of operation of government in relation to the way society distributes goods and services. Enabling means first of all to establish a clear framework of justice within which society can function and provide for itself the goods and services which are needed. The rules (like the rules of any good game), should be as clear as possible, but just as tough as is necessary to achieve the objective, which is in this case the maintenance of human rights.

There is another criterion of a good game which

25

applies equally to government. Once the game is set up, the rule-maker is unnecessary. You need an umpire to decide whether a player has broken a rule — but you do not have to keep on calling in the rule-maker to fill in the gaps, set up the courts, or provide you with balls. It should always be the general aim of government to make itself invisible and irrelevant in precisely this kind of way. The more it has to be called in to intervene, the worse it is doing its job.

Drawing up the rules of the game however is not sufficient on its own — especially in a society which has forgotten how to play. There is also a more positive side to the enabling role. There is often a need to 'oil the machinery' of social exchange — whether it is the market for goods and services, the setting up of new kinds of community organisation, or the normal activities of mutual support and self-help which have until recently been taken for granted. Much of the legislation we have grown up with makes it more and more complicated and difficult for people to take responsibility for their own lives, more and more necessary to leave everything to the large and safe institution. If any group tries to take back some responsibilities from the government institution — say in housing, health, transport — it will have a real mountaineering job to get over the legal obstacles erected, often with the best of motives, by the 'providers', and to contend with those whose jobs depend on providing. Enabling legislation would deliberately reverse this situation. It would begin by asking not 'how can we (the government) house all the people?', but 'how can we best enable people to provide for themselves the houses they need?'; not 'how can we (the government) employ all the people?', but 'how can we enable people to create work?'; not 'how can we (the government) provide care for all sick people?', but 'how can we enable people to take responsibility for their own health, and to cope with their disabilities?'

26

Finally, enabling must include *access* to resources. To enable must also mean to empower; and power depends on resources. Access to resources guaranteed by government must include access to those parts of the common heritage for which the government can be regarded as a trustee, such as the land, access to tools and capital and access to sufficient liquid assets in the form of cash to enable a person to meet basic needs.

PURCHASING AND PROVIDING

The exchange of goods and services by which society is maintained works formally through some kind of 'money' — money being a 'claim' on goods and services from society, in return for goods and services given to society by the individual. This is the basis of a sensible and just market economy. Some goods and services however benefit society as a whole, and in the case of such goods and services it is difficult to rely on an individualised marketing system because in an important sense everyone is a customer. Typically this is true of defence, the prevention of infectious diseases, or the fire brigade.

Now in this category of goods and services which are of general benefit, and in which individual customers cannot readily be identified, it is obviously sensible that the *people as a group* should purchase the goods or services which as a group they need. This purchasing should be done on whatever scale is appropriate — it could for instance be done on the scale of world, in the case of prevention of some infectious diseases, or it could be done on the scale of village, in the case of the fire brigade; but as a general rule, there is a choice of scale, and the smaller the scale, the more efficient the system. This is because the smaller the circle between payment and provision, the clearer the accountability, and the less the danger of slippage. If we pay for a World Health Organisation (WHO) to prevent infectious disease, it is very difficult for us to observe and control the outcome; if we pay for a village fire brigade, it is very easy to do so. The smaller the circle of accountability, the more the transaction resembles a sensible and just market model, where the individual purchaser can see and comprehend what he purchases.

However, on whatever scale the 'public' purchasing operates, then unless it is on such a small scale that it can be done round the village pump there must be some group to which the purchasing activity is delegated — a village committee, a government department, a board of trustees, the United Nations; and according to democratic principles, this group should be elected directly or indirectly on a one man one vote system. What has this got to do with government?

First of all, the case for communal purchasing of goods and services, which is quite straightforward, certainly does not constitute a case for communal *provision* of goods and services. If you delegate to a committee the job of purchasing an article of equipment, like a lawn-mower for the golf club, you would be rightly suspicious if the committee purchased the lawn-mower from one of its own members, and even more suspicious if it duplicated itself into a lawn-mower purchasing committee and a lawn-mower selling committee, and held incestuous bargaining sessions with itself.

Yet because of the identification of government with communal purchasing, and the further confusion of purchasing with provision, most 'public services' operate in precisely this way, with predictable inefficiency and irresponsibility. In the United States there has been a steady shift from direct municipal refuse collection to collection by private firms on contract to the municipality, and in some cases to totally private systems. A recent study made by the University of Columbia concluded that in every case private collection was superior to direct labour, and that savings amounted to up to 60% even on published municipal figures, although these figures ignored all kinds of overhead costs which a private firm would have to take into account.

The case for 'contracting' out all manner of provision for the elderly, the disabled and the sick is equally overwhelming, not only on grounds of economy but on grounds of humanity. Provision of services for the sick by family and friends is often the best possible system, and the governmental task then becomes that of ensuring that such care can take place rather than providing costly alternatives. In Wiltshire, the Social Services Department has taken the initiative of making small grants to community based day care associations for the elderly and infirm, involving extensive use of village halls and local volunteers. This has proved to be a clear alternative to residential provision at thirty times the cost — and the gain in happiness, community involvement and responsibility is enormous.

Secondly, the task of communal purchasing does not have to be a government task at all. Any community (including the national or the international community), can set up a communal purchasing function for anything it likes — but the government does not have to do it. Government will of course continue to be involved in substantial communal purchasing activities; but it is important to separate out in theory the public purchasing function for three important reasons.

The first reason is that if the government is clearly seen as carrying out a distinct public purchasing function on behalf of the community — say in education, investment in industry, or defence — then we can begin to create better systems of accountability, as we would expect of any other delegated public purchaser. Accountability to the community through parliament and the civil service is remote. If someone is buying something on our behalf, there should be a close circle of accountability; we must know who is buying what, and in whose interests, and what alternative buys are possible.

The second is that the all important question of *scale* can then be considered on the grounds of what is appropriate, and not on the grounds of what fits in with the government structure. There could well be a case with rapidly developing technology for instance for international but non-governmental provision of telecommunications services — and indeed this is already growing. The existence of localised governmental services could be a hindrance to such development. On the other hand fire services could well operate on a more local basis. Again American experiments on 'contracting out' this service on a local basis have revealed enormous potential for saving and increased efficiency. Some private fire services, for instance, discovering that three-quarters of all calls are for small fires in litter bins, cars or gardens, now provide small 'attack trucks' manned by two people at a tenth of the cost of a full engine. In New Jersey, the community has purchased the services of a private local police force.

The third reason for disentangling the principle of communal purchasing is that we can see much more clearly that there are many cases where private and public benefit is *mixed*, and where it is sensible therefore to combine an element of public purchasing with an element of private purchasing. The railways are an obvious case in point, where the benefit to the individual traveller which is defined and marketable is combined with an element of general public benefit. This general benefit has been clearly proved by the inhabitants of Pickering in North Yorkshire, who as a result of purchasing a local line due to be 'chopped' by British Rail now have a thriving small town with an abundance of well-stocked shops and public houses, as well as a commercially viable railway owned by a community trust. Sir Peter Parker, Chairman of British Rail, wants to have the public benefit aspect clearly

30

separated from the private benefit aspect, and paid for out of the public purse by a conscious decision, leaving the railway company to run a business on a proper commercial basis.

There is nothing difficult about such an arrangement; but it depends on first disentangling the functions of communal and private purchasing. Many apparently intractable employment problems could in fact be solved in this way. Some important services are now neglected, while many people who could perform them are unemployed. Some of these services have a clear communal good element, which could be communally purchased — leaving the private element to be purchased in the market. Hedge-laying as an alternative to mechanised cutting could be promoted in this way, thus creating many jobs and greatly benefitting the environment.

Many people may feel uneasy when we use the hard 'market' language of purchasing and value for money about social and public things such as education and welfare. I believe this unease is a sign of a profound division of thinking in our society which we must overcome. People mistakenly believe that there is on the one hand, the world of commerce, industry, money and purchasing, which is essential but morally suspect; and on the other hand, the world of morally and socially good things, like social work, education, charity, a world occupied by people who don't have to worry about the nasty commercial world, on which they depend — much as the wife in her traditional role depends on the husband. Uneasily astride the division between two worlds are nationalised industries.

This division is exacerbated by the whole history of capitalism and the socialist rejection of it; and it cuts right down through our educational system, generating almost two breeds of person who regard each other with mutual distrust and subdued hostility. Clearly we have to get to the root of this problem and break the stereotypes before there can be any process of healing.

I began by saying that in any society goods and services are produced or offered, and exchanged or purchased. This applies equally to privately purchased or communally purchased goods and services. There can be only one sensible reason for purchasing anything, and that is because the purchaser thinks it is a good buy — good in relation to the ends of values he or she or they wish to realise; and this also applies just as much to communal as to private purchasing. These ends may vary as much as human beings vary. In the morning I buy bacon and eggs in a cafe, in the evening I go to the theatre; this is private purchasing; the next day I pay my rates, and if I have a good local authority it lists what services I am communally 'buying'; this is communal purchasing, and the theory is that I can change the shopping list long-term by voting in collaboration with my fellow citizens. There is no difference between communal and private purchasing as regards the intrinsic value of what is being purchased. The only important question is what is the most appropriate purchasing system.

Similarly on the part of those offering or providing goods or services there should be no difference in principle between the public and the private sector. There can only be one reason for offering goods or services; that we believe they are of value, and that people (acting communally or individually) will purchase them, because they are of value to them. Teachers, social workers, civil servants, University professors, military Chiefs of Staff and M.P.s, are all marketing their services. They are marketing them at present to the general public through a very bad marketing system. But let us not make something mystical about what is being offered that obliges us to take it on faith. Many of the problems of the so-called 'mixed economy' come from first defining two systems that have opposing principles (one functioning for the public good and the other for private gain), and then finding that their principles conflict. It might be better to question the starting point.

EQUALITY

We have seen that equality is the keystone of the human rights tradition and of the first article of the Universal Declaration of Human Rights —

> All human beings are born free and equal in dignity and rights. They are endowed with reason and conscience and should act towards one another in a spirit of brotherhood.

Yet when equality is publicised as a political goal, most people's reactions are confused. On the one hand, we feel that equality is a noble ideal and central to our moral tradition; and we feel it is a scandal that the poor should starve while rich live in luxury. We therefore feel strongly drawn towards the principle of equality. On the other hand, equality conjures up a picture of dull uniformity and Procrustean harshness, cutting everyone down to size. Both of the reactions are legitimate; and the way to resolve the conflict is to think more clearly about what equality means, and what it ought to mean as a foundation for political action.

First of all it is important to dismiss some common interpretations of equality which are easy to fall into, and yet which on examination can be seen not to make sense. The commonest of these interpretations is to think of equality as 'equality of holdings', that is equality of things possessed.

Let us just think for a moment about the just society as implied by this interpretation. A just society would consist of a society in which everyone had equivalent holdings; to simplify, let us imagine a community of a hundred people shipwrecked on a desert island, and we have to share out provisions among them. By good fortune, we have a hundred barrels of beer, 200 loaves of bread, and 500 tins of baked beans. There seems to be an obvious just distribution on the principle of equality of holdings — everyone has a barrel of beer, two loaves, and 5 tins of baked beans. But what then? If individuals really *have* these things, that means they can dispose of them. Some will consume, some will save, some will barter, some will give, some may even lose their tins of beans — in other words, the whole complex system of human exchange will establish itself, and the essential variety of human beings will soon become mirrored in the variety of holdings.

What of the pattern of holdings or 'distribution' which results from this process? Do we have to say that is unjust, because it offends against the principle of equality? But if we say this, we have to say that the just system we started *inevitably* leads to an unjust system, because *having* things does not make any sense if we cannot to a large extent choose what to do with them. The only way to avoid this dilemma is to say that all the beer, bread and beans remain centrally owned, and that every day a beer official and bread official and beans official come round with a ration and make sure it is consumed by each individual.

We may on the other hand try to find a logical way

34

out by saying that the distribution system has *become* unequal and therefore unjust, but that we will 'rectify' it by redistributing. But how long should we leave the unjust pattern in existence before we rectify it? If equality of holdings is the foundation, why not immediately cancel out all forms of trading or exchange or giving or losing which spoil the pattern — thus effectively removing from our islanders any rights to what we have 'given' them?

Although this may seem a crude and highly abstract illustration, I believe it offers insights which could correct popular misconceptions about equality, and in particular about how it relates to liberty and self-determination. For this parable of the islanders not only holds as a critique of the crude egalitarian theory that everyone should have the same 'holdings', it holds equally well as a critique of any preconceived patterned system of holdings which is considered to be just at a certain point in time. Instead of saying everyone should have the same, we might say everyone should have an amount proportional to their size — or proportional to their merits — or proportional to their need; or we could work out a complicated mathematical equation that took into account size, merit and need. But however complicated we made our pattern, it would still go wrong as soon as people started to function freely within it, and would still lead to the same contradictions — or towards the same grotesque totalitarianism.*

---

* One of the most sophisticated and celebrated works in political philosophy to emerge in recent years has been John Rawls' 'Theory of Justice', which erects a system of distributive justice on the basis of the principles which a group of individuals would choose if they were meeting in complete abstraction from everything they know about themselves; while making the choice of principles, no-one knows about his position, social status, or natural assets and abilities; the principles of justice are thus chosen 'behind a veil of ignorance'. People in this situation, Rawls argues, would agree on two basic principles — one being equality of rights and duties, and the other being that social and economic inequalities were just only if they resulted in the least advantaged being better off than they would be without the inequalities. Rawls' subtle thesis still suffers from the objections we have raised to any 'patterned' and statistical conception of justice, in that it would immediately be undone by any process involving human freedom.

There is also another problem about any theory of justice which begins with a total abstraction from history and from human reality. Justice is to do with real people in real situations with a history. If we abstract totally from this, as did most of the natural law theorists of the Enlightenment, we conceive of individuals existing as pure intelligence, or abstract identities confronting the world. From such a basis we can only draw conclusions which treat people as identical, interchangeable parts (like bits of a machine), because it is our concreteness, our bodies and our histories that make us different. All the philosophies that develop from such abstract and defined concepts about what people are tend either towards total individualism, because it is through our bodies and our history and our individuality that we share; or towards an equally complete totalitarianism, but it is only through our bodies that we are individual people, with differences which prevent us ever being reduced to statistical abstractions. There is therefore a close philosophical link between total individualism and total state control.

But what about our original idea of sharing out the barrels of beer, tins of beans and loaves of bread among the shipwrecked islanders? Surely it is right and fair to share the goods out equally, or at least on some easily understood 'patterned' basis.

Of course it is sensible. But we must be careful about analogies. The island image is already loaded because it assumes that the group, or some central distributor has a right to dispose of all the goods, and a need for a rule of thumb to work by. This position is commonplace; we often have to divide a cake among a family, or share out chips (— the ones that go with with fish) and we need a similar rule of thumb. Equal shares is a good down-to-earth conflict-resolution technique — no more and no less. The same applies to the queue system — 'first come, first served'. It is an immediately intelligible rule of thumb, and therefore

36

a good technique to apply where there is no point in wasting time in endless wrangles.

It is dangerous however to extend this to a universal rule of distributive justice. The very word 'distributive justice' is loaded, because it suggests, like the island story, there is a distributor who has a right to dispose of everything. But it is precisely this point which needs to be questioned. If we begin by assuming that in any human society the community as a whole, or some central body representing it *owns everything*, then inevitably any conclusion we come to will reinforce this preconception; as it happens it is this preconception that is one of the tap-roots of totalitarianism. For if the state owns everything, the people own nothing; and whereas we might agree for instance that people should not 'own', in an absolute sense, common assets such as the air and the land, if we say that everything is owned by a central distributor we are on a very dangerous and slippery slope. What about our homes? What about the products of our labour? What about our talents? What about our heads? Are they one part of a common pool of resources? If not, where do we draw the line? This is an illustration of the danger of totalitarianism which is built into the premises of those theories of justice which begin by separating the individual from his history and his body, from his 'existential density', and end by annihilating him altogether in a rational machine in which people are numbers.

If equality of *holdings* is an illusory principle, as we have argued, can we say that equality of *opportunity* is a more valid objective? Unfortunately, equality of opportunity in any measurable sense would have to be tied to equality in holdings, and therefore can have no more practical basis than the first principle. And as with the equal holdings principle, we can soon find ourselves taking absurd positions if we try to equalise opportunity. Opportunity to what? To sunshine — an important element in health and well-being? To avoiding accidental death? To marrying the Prince of Wales? None of these is a trivial objective, but the idea of equalising opportunity in relation to them is mind-boggling. The appeal of the idea of equality of opportunity however needs to be examined, because it is based on a sense of fairness.

If society is visualised as a race, with everyone competing for the same prize, or as a pyramid, with everyone trying to get to the top, then certainly there must be some kind of rule about equal opportunity. It would be unfair if one person started nearer the winning post, or someone else started with only one leg. What we have to question however is the whole race or pyramid analogy. Society does *not* consist of many people competing for the same goal, and there is no adjudicator or prize. Individuals might choose to structure their lives like this, and imagine it to be the case. But society as a whole manifestly is not like this, but is a complex pattern of immensely varied individuals pursuing immensely varied goals, and entering into all kinds of exchange relationships with each other in doing so.

The idea of a pyramid society is in fact a profound contradiction of one aspect of equality which we must accept. And this is equality of respect. Looking back at the Universal Declaration of Human Rights, we find that what is actually stated is that human beings are equal in *dignity* and *rights*. These two words are useful starting points for a more positive understanding.

The pyramid concept of society is a myth which destroys the very roots of democracy in the minds and hearts of the people living in a democratic society. If equality of opportunity means an equal chance to get to the top, an equal chance to push everyone else off on the way up, and an equal chance to dominate all those below, then far from being a principle of equality, it is a principle of domination. It reinforces unjust power structures by cloaking them with

38

morality and encourages the self-made tyrant to see himself as a paragon of virtue.

If human beings are equal in *dignity*, this implies that they must deserve equal *respect*, for dignity justifies respect. Difficult as this concept is to define, it has profound implications. It is basically to do with how people relate to each other. It does not mean that everyone has an equal chance to climb the pyramid, but that in a radical sense there *is no pyramid*. There can of course be *functional* pyramids, organisational pyramids, and these are as necessary to business as they are to football teams; but if there is equality of respect, there can by definition be no *pyramid of respect*. In the words of the Universal Declaration of Human Rights, 'we should treat one another as brothers'. Whether we see a prince or a pauper, a starving child or a Prime Minister, we know they must command equal *respect*. It is a hard way to live, and impossible to quantify, but terrifying in its implications. It cannot be written into a political programme; but it is political dynamite.

What then can be written into a political programme? The second phrase in the Declaration article provides the clue; equality of *rights* can be written into a programme. Equality of rights is no more than the gradual working out through history of the principle of equality of respect. The two are inseparable. Equality of respect is in danger of remaining a comfortable illusion until it becomes a commitment to equality of rights. This commitment to equality of rights in turn transfigures the meaning of equality of respect.

As human rights are progressively realised in society, behaviour is changed and hence perceptions are changed; we see people differently, and this means people *are* different, because you cannot separate people from the way they perceive each other and behave towards each other. Respect *creates* dignity, and this relationship is reinforced by rights. For instance, in a society where the norm was slavery, or apartheid, perceptions would be different. Unenslaveable is for us part of the very essence of being a person, just as 'unkillable' is. That is why in modern warfare people tend to dehumanise the enemy, in order to strip him of his most fundamental rights.

As the scope of human rights extend, to include the economic, social, political and civil rights already in the process of development, so our very perception of people will change — and people themselves will change. These rights will become part of the characteristics of being a person. This is where equality finds its real basis. We cannot define any human right without saying at the same time that this is a right of all human beings — otherwise it is not a human right, but a British right, or a white man's right, or something else. What this equality of right means in concrete terms must be worked out in each society, or in the international community itself, through historical process. But an equal right certainly should not be quantified and therefore trivialised into a right to an equal *quantity* of anything at all. An equal right to a home is not a right to an equal home; an equal right to work is not a right to equal work; and, for that matter, an equal right to life is not a right to an 'equal' life, whatever that might mean.

What then of the scandal of inequality with which we began? Is it not shameful that the poor should starve while the rich live in luxury? Is not the elimination of poverty a prime aim of a just government? Indeed it is. It is a prime duty of government to eliminate poverty, which implies the denial of human rights in our society. I will argue later the case for a basic social wage which I believe is the right way at this time to achieve this result.

It should also be the continuous duty of government to combat and neutralise large accumulations of wealth and power which encroach on the rights of people, as for instance by taxation and anti-monopoly legislation. It is a fact verified by history and common experience that wealth and power tend to be self-
40

generating; 'to him that hath shall be given'. In the light of this tendency, and the possibility of domination in defiance of human rights which it implies, there is a continuous remedial task to be carried out which no legitimate government can avoid. It is vital however that the future role of government in the progressive realisation of human rights should not become identified with the pursuit of equality in the statistical 'levelling' sense, which we have seen to be both ill-founded and dangerous; for this could only lead to a denial of those human rights of which equality, in its true sense, is the vital principle.

Summary

I have argued that the purpose of government should be to promote and maintain basic human rights, and that these rights are related to the needs on which human fulfilment depends. Human communities are not however just raw material or clay lying about and waiting to be organised into human rights form. They are complex living systems in which goods and services are continuously exchanged, both individually and communally, to meet basic needs. It is essential therefore that government should not confuse the job of maintaining rights with that of providing or of communal purchasing. Its job is rather to enable rather than to provide or purchase. Equality of rights is the foundation of justice, but must not be identified with equal holdings or with equal opportunity.

In the following chapters I will look at some key policy areas — work, housing, energy and defence — to see how these general principles can be applied.

Chapter Three
WORK: THE FORMAL ECONOMY

WHAT IS THE RIGHT TO WORK?

All rights are based on fundamental human needs. What then are the needs on which the right to work is based?

It is easy to think that people work because they have to 'earn a living'; yet the experience of many who are thrown out of work (or who retire prematurely) suggests that when work goes, the meaning of life goes too. Work is not just a means to an end, it is part of the essential texture of human existence.

One aspect of work is the need to *belong*. This belonging can mean two things. It can mean being part of a working group, a working community; and it can mean making a contribution to society, which society acknowledges, normally (but not necessarily) through payment. Work is a contract with society, which gives an individual an assurance of being an accepted and participating member of the community.

Another vital aspect of work is the development of skills and talents, which brings immense satisfaction, especially again when the skills and talents are socially recognised and rewarded. Closely connected with this is the need to *create*. People express themselves in

42

their work; it is part of themselves, a kind of self-realisation. This self-realisation is at its highest point in the skilled craftsman or the artist, but it is an experience which everyone shares.

The experience of unemployment proves that the right to work is based on a fundamental human need. This experience is for most people deeply distressing — quite apart from consequent hardships such as the deterioration of family life, loss of status and loss of friends. The root cause of the distress is rather the sense of not being needed — of being 'on the scrap heap' without a social identity. For the young, who have not yet had jobs, this is the most damaging and dangerous experience we can possibly inflict upon them. Damaging, because it means they do not form their social bond with the community which is symbolised in our society by 'having a job', with the give-and-take which that implies; and dangerous, because young people who are cut off in this way from the main body of society really have only two behaviour choices open to them — apathy or aggression.*

Technically the right to work is now well-established in international law, especially in Article 6 of the International Covenant on Economic, Social and Cultural Rights, which reads as follows:

> The States Parties to the present Covenant recognise the right of everyone to the opportunities to gain his living by work which he freely chooses and accepts, and will take appropriate steps to safeguard this right.

The term 'work' is not closely defined. It obviously must exclude all forms of forced labour (which are declared elsewhere to be contrary to human rights). Work must be *freely chosen or accepted*; and it must be remunerated in a way which provides a decent standard of living in accord with the rest of the provisions of the covenant (Article 7).

* Eisenberg P. & Lazarsfeld P. F. (1938) 'The Psychological Effects of Unemployment', *Psychological Bulletin 35*. This article lists 112 studies demonstrating these effects, which have been confirmed by subsequent research.

On the other hand, work is certainly not the same as employment. Employment is a particular kind of contract to exchange labour for money — carelessly identified with work because it is a very common form of contract in modern industrial society. Yet we know that many work and are not employed; and, for that matter, that many are employed and do not work!

It could be objected at this stage that the 'legal' right to work is nonsense, for at least two reasons. First of all it cannot be enforced; and secondly, because governments that have signed the Covenant have certainly not taken it seriously, since their practice has totally contradicted the theory. There is much truth in this, but it would be a mistake all the same to dismiss the formal legal commitment too lightly. The covenants were not lightly signed; and they provide a basis on which a political campaign can be built. Paper commitments can easily acquire a force not foreseen at the time of signing, especially if the commitment has a strong basis in a common sense of justice. This is the case with the right to work.

THE PROBLEM

CHANGING PATTERN OF WORK*

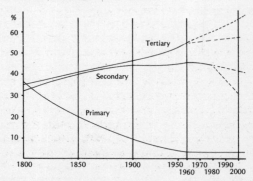

* Diagram reproduced from *Our Secret Economy*, Graeme Shankland, Anglo-German Foundation 1980, by kind permission of the author.

44

There is obviously a serious breakdown in the system through which people realise their right to work in our society. To understand this breakdown, we need to take a broad historical view.

Employment is traditionally divided into three categories — primary, secondary and tertiary. Primary employment is to do with extracting materials from the earth which are useful to man — mainly agriculture and mining. Secondary is to do with transforming these materials by manufacturing processes. Tertiary is all the rest — mainly the 'service sector' — professionals, clerical, insurance and banking, retailing, transport and communications — which keeps the whole system functioning.

Half the working population at the beginning of the industrial revolution were in primary employment — mostly on the land. The effect of industrialisation has been to reduce this to one twentieth. Most of those leaving primary production were absorbed into secondary production — the manufacturing process. Now the number engaged in manufacturing is declining rapidly, and all evidence suggests that less and less people will be required to produce more and more of the standard manufactured products (like cars) which we take for granted as the basis of our way of life.

Many people argued until recently that the third sector, the services sector, would increase and take up all the slack. Yet many services which were previously provided from outside the household are increasingly replaced by production within the household using goods, essentially capital goods (like washing machines) acquired from manufacturing industry.

Of greater significance is the impact of the microprocessor which could eliminate at a stroke the majority of routine clerical jobs. The micro-chip heralds a second 'industrial revolution'. Optimists argue that the loss of jobs resulting from automation will be made up by new industrial developments based on micro-technology, and by the release of other wealth

45

for the purchase of other products as automated manufacture reduces prices. So some extent this will happen; but Fiat's new automated production line, typical of the revolution in manufacturing, requires 25 instead of 126 people to operate it; and in the service and information industries (including all clerical jobs), which occupies half the work force in the country, the Association of Scientific Technical & Managerial Staff (ASTMS) (though perhaps a biased source), forecasts a loss of 2.6 million jobs by 1985. New jobs created are not likely automatically to 'mop up' this unemployment — particularly as the new jobs will tend to be highly skilled, or in many cases in quite different parts of the world from those where the job loss has its worst impact.

Another underlying cause of unemployment is the necessarily changing position of British products in the world trading scheme. Our steel industry for instance was created at a time when Britain was the major world producer and exporter of steel exchanged for raw material imported from all over the world. Now this position is radically changed as steel production takes place throughout the world, often far from the raw materials source, and Britain is only one of a number of producers now forced to reduce in size and specialise. The same argument applies in general terms to a whole field of manufactured goods, such as textiles or motor vehicles, in which Britain once led the world, but is now having to take her place as one of a large and growing number of exporting countries.

If it is true (and of course there can be differing views) that these underlying causes (or others) are operating to produce large-scale unemployment in industrialised countries, then the government has a very great responsibility in this field. Its responsibility is not that of a general manager, or a Super-Board of Directors. Its job is to maintain the right to work; and in carrying out this job it should act in its primary

46

role as legislator and in its secondary role as public purchaser; not if it can be avoided as a provider or a manager.

MISTAKEN STRATEGIES

In this situation, how might a government approach its task of maintaining the right to work? First we have to dismiss some policies which obviously don't fit the bill.

Relying on the Market

One such policy is to say that market forces will eventually solve the problem, and that government should keep out of the way. Market forces unfortunately will not resolve the work problem in a way that respects human rights. The main reason for this is the enormous scale of modern industrial organisation and the concentration of workers as employees in certain localities and in certain industries, which are indeed subject to massive and long-term market forces — but these forces may well result in devastating whole communities by abruptly depriving them of their principle means of livelihood. The hidden hand of the market is an excellent and skilful operator; but while admiring the work of the hidden hand, we have to ensure that human rights are protected from the hob-nailed boot of the hidden foot!

Planning the Economy

The opposite extreme to be avoided is the planner's paradise. It is the policy of massive intervention in the whole industrial process, so that central government controls, fosters, encourages, manages, through devices such as planning agreements, development certificates, subsidies and grants, thereby benevolently guiding the whole economic process in such a way that all needs are met, including the need for work. This approach is first of all too vast and too unfocussed in both aim and method; and secondly, it depends

47

on a detailed knowledge of how the economy works, and of which levers to pull at what time, which is quite clearly not available to government or anyone else, and probably never will be. The history of the abortive efforts at wholesale industrial planning in the Eastern as well as the Western world during the past 20 years sufficiently proves the point.*

Because of the unsatisfactory nature of this second policy, there is a stronger and more frightening version of it waiting in the wings. It could always be argued that *real* planning has never been tried — planning of markets, prices, consumption — for that matter, direction of labour. After all, the unemployment problem could quite easily be resolved by reintroducing military service. In this direction lies a totalitarianism which provides an empty shell of a right to work, without the kernel of self-determination which is its life principle. The doctrinaire interventionists and the doctrinaire non-interventionists have one thing in common; neither has a doctrine. Neither has asked what government intervention is *for*; both adopt irrational positions because they support a method without first defining an objective.

Government intervention in industry has a simple and clearly defined purpose, and that is to guarantee the right to work. There are a few other clear grounds for intervention, which will be discussed elsewhere.

Growth

A third mistaken strategy is to say that the only way for the government to guarantee human rights, including the right to work, is to make the economy grow, in the sense of increasing the Gross National Product (GNP). If the economy grows, it is argued, jobs will be created for the unemployed, and taxes will be generated so that government can pay for education and welfare. Therefore the government's first aim must be to make the economy grow.

* See *The Politics of Planning* by Alan Budd, Fontana, 1978.

This approach however makes a number of questionable assumptions.

Does the government need a great deal more money in order to meet its obligations? The government's primary job is not to provide but to enable, and a *gradual* switch to such a policy would involve a large and ever-increasing saving of public funds. Policies for encouraging small firms for instance generate far more revenue than they would cost.

Does it follow that if the economy grows the problem of unemployment will disappear? Evidently not. The growth of the economy in the next phase of industrial society is likely to involve heavy investment in labour-saving technology and could therefore make the problem worse.

The experience of developing countries can help us to understand the difference between promoting economic growth and promoting human rights, including the right to work. In the 1950s, the Germans introduced a large plastic sandal factory into Egypt. As a direct consequence, hundreds of leather craftsmen were deprived of their work; village economies declined and people eventually had to spend more for their footwear because plastic sandals don't last and cannot be repaired! Yet growth in the economy had occurred. In Sri Lanka, there is now a powerful non-governmental village development movement (Sarvodaya), which bases its policy on what the people actually need. In thousands of villages, the people were asked to place their needs in order of priority. High on the list came family ties, social contact, roads, clean water; below came economic development. They rejected developments like centralised food-processing or metalworking factories which destroyed village skills and social structure.

The underlying objection to the 'economy first, values second' argument however is that it is a debasement of the function of government. If getting the economy right comes first, getting the economy right

49

will come last as well, and what will be obscured is that politics is about values and the promotion of human rights. The satirist Jonathan Swift once made a 'Modest Proposal' for solving the problems of the Irish economy; since there were too many babies and too little food, he proposed that the poor should sell their surplus babies to the rich for food, thus solving both problems at once. In a similar vein, a Welsh comedian, commenting on a proposal to build a new slaughterhouse in South Wales, welcomed in on the grounds that a slaughterhouse could solve the problems of South Wales 'at a stroke'!

Economic problems look different in the mirror of human rights.

All this certainly does not mean that economic growth is bad. Most firms see growth in terms of the balance sheet as a prime objective, and they have every right to do so; and they have every right to demand that the government enables them to pursue this objective, provided it does not conflict with the people's rights. Then the firm's objective is to grow. The government's job is to ensure that the firm's successes and failures take place within a general context of justice and human rights.

To illustrate the point, it is quite easy to imagine a country (there are several in South America) where there is explosive economic growth, and where there is a gangster government in the hands of a self-appointed elite, which systematically imprisons, tortures and generally overrides the fundamental human rights of a substantial proportion of the people. Such a government would not qualify as a government at all according to the definition we propose. On the other hand, we can equally well imagine a society where people have made an option not to grow economically but rather to pursue other values within a stable economic framework; and one can also imagine that in this society everyone has a home, satisfying work, a reasonable standard of living, and is protected by a reliable system of justice. The government of such a country would be a good government, with or without growth.

Provision

A fourth mistaken strategy is for the government to *provide* work. There is much public purchasing to be done, which will result in more jobs being available.

'Making up' jobs and then providing them for people with public money (as with many of the programmes of the Manpower Services Commission), is not a proper way to promote the right to work. Like all forms of providing by government to meet basic rights, it tends to degrade the meaning of the right which is being protected — a bit like giving the children something to occupy them to keep them out of mischief. Similarly, like other forms of providing it tends to escalate out of control, or to come to a sudden halt, leaving people worse off than they were before.

Work must be 'real', and seen to be real; and there is an important sense in which work (like life) cannot be provided.

APPROPRIATE STRATEGIES — *The Moderating Function*

If some big industries are going downhill, and others going uphill, the government has the job of smoothing the downward path and smoothing the upward one. This can be called 'the moderating function'.

The aim of smoothing the downward path is that there should never be a large concentration of unemployed in one area, since this has the effect of virtually eliminating the right to work in that area. At the same time, a downward path must be recognised as a downward path in terms of quantity of jobs available (though this could well be accompanied by an improvement in quality of jobs); and there are a great many downward paths of this kind which are easy to identify.

Temporary subsidies may be the only way in some cases for the government to play its moderating role in a rapidly declining industry. It is like an ambulance service; when there is a serious accident, action must be taken regardless of cost and long-term policies. However, the occurrence of major accidents of this kind is a result of the failure of government to meet its objectives in more intelligent and far-sighted ways. Just as the railways investigate every major accident and make whatever design changes are required to avoid its recurrence, so in the light of employment accidents should the Government re-design its employment strategy.

Protection from overseas competition through tariffs may also be a necessary temporary measure, especially where overseas governments are also subsidising and protecting. It is wrong to be dogmatic about protection or anti-protection; but government needs to be dogmatic about the right to work. At the same time, protection like subsidies (in the 'propping-up' sense of the word) should be seen as part of the moderating role, and therefore temporary and on a declining scale *providing* a positive 'enabling' policy is adopted at the same time to foster new work opportunities. There is no basis for saying that it is the government's job to maintain existing industries, however big or important they are at present. Industries, like people, have no right to perpetual existence. We can wrap them round with embalmed cloths and build pyramids around them if we wish, but there may be better things to do with our resources.

Just as government may have a responsibility to smooth the downward path, so it has a responsibility in some cases to smooth the upward one. There are some major industrial and technological developments on the horizon which could offer promise of a large number of good quality work opportunities during the next twenty years. In most cases these new work opportunities will emerge without government intervention, simply by the operation of the market; but in other cases there could be arguments for oiling the market, on the basis of an assessment of future work opportunities. This assessment might lead in a number of different directions.

At one extreme an assessment of formal work opportunities in the year 2000 would indicate a substantial development in electronics, telecommunications, micro-processors, which to a small extent could offset the inevitable decline in traditional manufactures. From this point of view the National Enterprise Board's investment in Inmos makes sense. Investment by a public investment body established by the government in the long-term interests of society is a sensible means of exercising the government's responsibility to maintain the right to work. At the other extreme, this assessment might well indicate, for instance, that small-scale and less chemical-intensive agriculture would become increasingly viable as the cost of chemical farming increases. In that case, it would be important to increase training programmes in these fields, and encourage new enterprises to set up. Since one of the obstacles to changing from chemical to organic cultivation is the problem of *transition*, it would be important to make credit available to farmers for this transition period.

These two very different kinds of development have one thing in common; they are both economical in use of energy and raw materials. Any long-term assessment of work possibilities must take into account the role of government as trustee of resources. On 'spaceship earth', we have to move steadily from an industrial system which is wasteful of energy and materials to one which conserves them. This means in general that there must be more emphasis on the '4Rs' — Repair, Reconditioning, Re-use and Recyling. As it happens, all these activities are labour-intensive; old materials make new jobs. There are many ways in which Government should promote conservation and the 4Rs — for instance by shifting some of the tax burden from labour to materials.

The responsibility of government as a trustee of resources coincides neatly in this case with its responsibility to maintain the right to work.

Public Purchasing

Government is as we have seen responsible for a great deal of communal purchasing.

One of the extraordinary things about the present employment situation is that we have on the one hand a vast army of unemployed people receiving substantial payments from the public purse for doing nothing, and on the other hand we have an enormous need for public works to be carried out in our decaying urban and industrial areas. The public works that need to be done are by no means concerned with what could be dismissed as luxuries. To give only one example, the vast sewerage systems under many of our old industrial towns have now been in operation over a hundred years, and are far past their expected working lives. In many cases they are in an extremely dangerous state; in Manchester cavities have been known to open up which could swallow up a double decker bus.

The cost of renewing the sewerage system is so enormous that public authorities usually prefer not to start doing the sums. In fact, a serious assessment of the whole system in our large conurbations, taking into account normal replacement costs, would show that our whole sewage treatment system needs to be radically rethought on purely financial grounds.

Whatever course we take, however, involves a vast amount of work, most of it for the construction industry, which is of course exactly where there is also heavy unemployment. This is only one example of many. We only have to look round the decaying fabric of many industrial cities to realise the quantity of public work to be done which is essential as a basis

54

for future private or public development. Outside the cities the crumbling ruins of the industrial revolution and the blocked waterways and canals are crying out for imaginative development that could make them valuable assets for the future.

As a society we are a bit like a neurotic individual, who sits in a basically luxurious house surrounded by weeks of dirty washing up, decaying rubbish, and weed infested gardens, complaining that there is nothing to do.

The communal purchasing job is clearly not functioning properly. If economic theory leads us to defend this absurd state of affairs, then we must ask economists to find a new theory and release the energy of people to do the work that needs to be done.

In some cases (as in the capital-intensive 'public works' mentioned above), the public purchasing that needs to be done can only be done at present by government. In other cases, there can be a partnership between public and private purchasing, when a service is partly for the common good, and partly marketable to individuals.

In the Uplands Management Project in the Cumbria National Park, for instance, the Park Authority, in the interests of tourism, has agreed to pay a proportion of the labour costs of farmers wishing to construct walls, maintain paths or plant trees. This immediately increases the real work opportunities in the district, and enables farmers often to retain the full-time services of an employee who would otherwise be out of work in the winter. The beauty of the system is that it leaves the individual farmer completely free to make his own work contracts; it involves a minimum of bureaucracy; and instead of a 'subsidy' in the vague propping-up sense it involves a clearly defined communal purchasing function dovetailed into the labour market.

Public purchasing of this kind can both moderate

the impact of unemployment on declining sectors, and provide a significant boost to work opportunities in many sectors where the public good is partly involved.

Small Firms·

A third aspect of employment policy is the promotion of independent initiatives to provide goods and services — i.e. small firms or 'private enterprises'.

Because work has become identified with employment, most people today automatically think that a job is something you can only 'get' from an employer. They do not think of *making* a job, by offering a service or meeting a need themselves.

A shift of consciousness is required on this matter both in government and in the general public in order to perceive the enormous importance of small independent businesses both for the general economic health of a country and — our present concern — for the maintenance of the right to work.

If we think about 'the economy', we tend to think about the local large-scale industrial employer. Yet if we actually look around our town or village, and think about who in our local community is providing goods and services — including the shopkeepers, the professionals, the garages, the fish and chip shops, the builders the repairers, and a host of others, we will soon realise that a very substantial proportion of what is going on is in very small independent ventures. Much less obviously but equally important, is the fact that in any district at any point in time there is likely to be some new creative enterprise, some embryo of innovative development, which has promise of growing rapidly and creating wealth and job opportunities out of all proportion to the present size; and many of these will be very small, because small firms rather than large ones are the main centres of innovation in society.

In 1976 in the U.K., 6.21 million people were

employed in the small firms sector — nearly a quarter of the entire working population; and in the United States, it has been found that by far the major source of new job opportunities lies in the small firms sector.

It is however not just a quantity measurement that makes small firms important in relation to the right to work. There is also a quality dimension. At the core of all human rights including the right to work, is the principle of freedom and self-determination. A large proportion of people working in small firms have a very much greater degree of self-determination in their work than those employed in a large firm. They are more aware of the whole enterprise, and of the resources which it commands; and because of this, there is in general a greater degree of responsibility.

Small firms in comparison to large ones respond rapidly to change, are a major source of innovation, have a good industrial relations record, offer satisfying employment, are usually less capital intensive and are capable of operating with low overhead expenses. Moreover, they produce a bigger return on investments. Figures published in the Harvard Business Review for January/February 1979 show that over the whole range of business firms (manufacturing, services, construction, transportation and wholesale/retail) there is a steady and totally consistent decrease in earnings per dollar of invested assets as the quantity of assets increases. This seems to bear out a general rule of human behaviour, which anyone can check against his or her own experience. The rule is that the smaller the resource, the better it will be used (resource is defined as a means of benefit or fulfilment to a human agent over which he has control). Think of the use of space in a caravan — of soil in a small garden — or for that matter of the use of petrol in a small car!

If small firms are so vigorous, why is there a problem? The problem is that we live in a society which is

57

largely dominated by the needs of large firms, because these are visible and powerful. There is a strong bias in practically all our public institutions and in most of our legislation against the small and in favour of the large.

This is true in general of industrialised countries; but it is especially true of this country. The birth rate of small firms in Britain is lower than in any country in the western world.

A few examples will show how this bias works. It is in general much more difficult to raise small amounts of capital than large. Large investment institutions and commercial banks do not normally consider making small loans because the management costs are too high. Government training and advisory services for industry are geared almost entirely to the needs of large firms. Nearly all publicly financed management training is relevant only to the needs of large firms, which are thus being subsidised at the expense of the small. Purchasing departments both of public and the private sector large institutions relate naturally to large-scale suppliers even when local small suppliers could supply cheaper and better products. Planning policies can stifle the growth of small firms who have no resources to cope with an oppressive bureaucracy, whereas large firms have more resources to cope. Similarly other forms of governmental intervention in forms such as VAT and licencing weigh very much more heavily on the small firms, where everyone is likely to be working flat out to survive, than on the large firm where there is a comfortable cushioning of professional help.

This bias in society should be systematically reversed, and a bold and adventurous programme in this field is essential if the work-creating potential of the small-scale economy is to be realised. The first job is to make sure the rules of the game work to help rather than hinder small initiatives. This means getting rid of unnecessary constraints and vexatious legislation

58

particularly in the field of planning and building regulations. The right to work is more basic than the right to a certain size of window or access road.

The second job is to correct the bias of the present structure which works against the small and in favour of the large. Public funds can be used to guarantee loans from banks for small business. This guarantee could be seen as a sensible public purchasing function on commercial grounds alone, since the public as a whole benefits greatly from the value added by small firms. Individuals can be entitled to tax relief on funds invested in a small business. Such measures would increase the flow of funds in a decentralised way, without an increase in bureaucracy. A more radical, more effective, and even more decentralised system would however be established by a switch from income tax to expenditure tax. By effectively exempting investment from tax, expenditure taxation would release much of the vast personal resources at present locked up in savings and pension funds, and encourage people to 'back' themselves or others in new ventures, either individually or through an intermediary fund.*

It is important for small firms to build up a working capital in the early years. Working capital is the financial 'tool' of the small business — just as necessary as any other piece of equipment. It is counter-productive even for the Exchequer to have a taxation system which makes it difficult to acquire this tool. In the early years, a businessman is confronted simultaneously with the tasks of supporting himself, building a working fund, and paying substantial sums to the taxman. A tax holiday in the early years would relieve this pressure — though again, a shift to expenditure tax would be a more radical and more effective solution.

* For a full account of the possibilities of an Expenditure Tax see *The Structure and Reform of Direct Taxation*, Report of a Committee chaired by Professor J. E. Meade, Institute for Fiscal Studies 1977.

Finally, there is the question of education, training, supporting and advisory services of all kinds. If small firms were supported with public funds in these fields in the same way as large firms, and in proportion to their contribution to the creation of work, every town would have publicly purchased services of the highest quality to offer to the small businessman. Schools and colleges can play an important part in bringing about the change of consciousness that is needed. Some High Schools in the U.S.A. incorporate along the school corridor barbers shops, restaurants, metalwork shops, dry cleaners and day-care centres, still run by students. The London Business School is now taking a similar initiative to enable students to run small businesses in nearby premises as part of their course.

Some idea of the effect that could be produced by a vigorous policy of this kind is given in an article in the Financial Times (29th October 1980). The article describes what has already been achieved in Japan. There are now seven million small firms in Japan, averaging between five and six employees. (Imagine, every sixth worker is a company president!) Up to the end of the second World War small companies were out of favour in Japan. But since 1948 they have been a central feature of industrial policy, encouraged by the creation of a Small and Medium Size Enterprise Agency. Laws were introduced to provide for tax deferrals to encourage modernisation, consulting services, and exemption from anti-monopoly legislation. Government sponsored financial institutions and private credit guarantee associations were established and tax breaks on corporate income below a level of 7m Yen were introduced. The result has been that for every 3 Japanese small firms that fail, 3.5 new ones are created; and while employment in the whole manufacturing sector declines, the share of the small companies sector has been increasing. Toyota's 140 direct suppliers draw upon 40,000

60

sub-contractors who contribute 60% of Toyota's parts.

COST OF EMPLOYMENT

A question that is bound to arise in people's minds when we talk about the 'right to work' is the frightening scale of the problem, and therefore the frightening costs of any government initiative that can make any impact. It is important to consider the cost element, because it illustrates an important aspect of the human rights approach.

When calculating the public cost of measures to combat unemployment we have to consider the public cost of unemployment itself. A Treasury estimate* puts the cost to the Exchequer of each unemployed worker at £3,500 p.a. — made up of lost tax receipts and National Insurance contributions, plus national insurance and other benefits and the cost of staff to administer these. A T.U.C. estimate published in January does a similar sum in relation to a typical family with two children on £6,000 p.a. income and finds that the cost to the public of unemployment for the family is £6,207 p.a.

Why is this so? Have government policy makers just been unfairly caught in a trap with no way out? Or are they victims of some inexorable law of economics? Not at all. Policy makers are caught in a moral commitment. We have decided, as a community, that people in this country have an unchallengeable right to a certain basic standard of living; we have decided, as a community acting through political processes, that we do not wish to live in a society where a large proportion of the population are forced to beg or starve. This is not an economic law; it is a choice. It is a choice which has very difficult economic consequences. It is highly inconvenient that the present government's deflationary policy leads directly to a

* *Economic Progress Report no. 130*, available free from the Information Division, H.M. Treasury, Parliament Street, London SW1.

huge charge on the Exchequer, and hence to inflation-
ary borrowing. Nevertheless, no politician has come
up with a 'modest proposal' to abolish payments to
the unemployed for economic reasons.

Just as we have made a commitment to the right
to freedom from hunger and poverty, so we can and
should accept a commitment to the right to work.
We are already committed to the 'expensive' human
right of freedom from want; fulfilment of the right
to real work would immensely increase the real wealth
of the community.

Chapter Four
WORK: THE INFORMAL ECONOMY

THE FORMAL AND INFORMAL ECONOMIES

Employment in the 'formal' economy — which shows up in national statistics, consists of full-time 'jobs' in the public or private sectors. But employment in this sense is not all that we *mean* when we use the word work. There is admittedly a tendency for the two words to be carelessly interchanged; but they are clearly not the same. What else goes on in society that is 'work' besides work in the formal economy?

There is a staggering omission from traditional economic thinking; and that is the household economy, including what is usually characterised as 'women's work'. The scale of this omission is so huge that when people see it for the first time, it is like the miracle of the blind suddenly seeing! We can make an approximate calculation of the order of magnitude involved by a simple wage calculation. If we assume there are 10 million housewives or househusbands in Britain, and that their work is worth a modest £4,000 p.a., the total labour of these people alone is worth £40 *billion* — 28% of the G.N.P.!

Why do we ignore this? Because it is trivial? The household is the place where all the basic caring services are provided for the majority of the population, and where the next generation of human beings are formed. This work is hardly trivial. It is odd that we have thought ourselves into a situation where a man is considered to be working if he spends his day in an office designing an advertisement for a new type of cornflake, and the woman who runs the whole domestic economy is considered in some strange sense to be not 'working'!

Historically, before the industrial revolution, most production of goods as well as services was carried out within the domestic economy. Much economic activity was then *transferred* to the market place and only then was recorded, so that for instance the woman who bottled fruit at home which the family ate was not part of 'the economy', but when she went to work in a canning factory and bought tins she entered the 'economy'; and behold there was growth! She also added to 'the economy' by her need for transport, and by her need for extra rubbish collection to take away the tins. A great deal of this growth is therefore a statistical illusion. We are now again in a phase where there is a lot of transferring going on in both directions between the household economy and the market economy; and if we just see this in terms of growth or decline of 'the economy' we are half blind to reality.

Obviously the reason why the household economy is not counted is literally that it cannot be 'counted'; it does not use money. But money is merely a tool — it is the shadow of the real economy, not the substance. The substance is work and the creation and exchange of goods and services for human benefit. The arbitrary nature of the divide between the market and the household economies can be illustrated by a 'modest proposal' for increasing the G.N.P. by 28% overnight. All housewives could go to work next door, and pay each other large salaries. These salaries could be then recorded in the G.N.P., though no one would be any the better off (except, unfortunately, the Exchequer)!

It is not just a question of labour. A group of economists in the United States carried out in the 1960s a survey of investment in 'consumer durables' in the household — laundry equipment, TVs, cars, etc; they then calculated the imputed return on investment, assuming that without this equipment services would have to be purchased. The total return on investment was found to be $16 billion, and it appeared that the household economy was accumulating physical wealth faster than the total corporate economy of the United States!*

Having broken the mould of stereotyped thinking about 'the economy', we can take a fresh look at all the other areas of work in a perfectly valid sense which are not 'employment' in the formal economy. In order to identify some important areas, it is useful to think about what most people do with their time. There are 168 hours in a week, and if we are 'in work' we may be employed for 40 of them, and sleep for 50. What of the other 78? Some is 'play'; but a good deal I expect we would prefer to call work — not all of it on the household economy. Other large areas of work outside the formal economy include for instance all kinds of self-help, service to others, and voluntary work. Politicians should be the last to underestimate this last category because the whole machinery of all

* *The Household Economy* (originally *Home Inc.*) Scott Burns, Beacon Press, Boston, U.S.A. (1977).

political parties, and all new movements depends entirely upon voluntary work!

Between the formal and the informal economies there is the 'grey' area where the informal economy merges with the formal — and this merging causes problems we shall discuss later. There is the world of 'odd jobbing' — part-time paid work, barter, moonlighting — the standard economy in some rural areas. In this area money is used (sometimes in a very 'informal' way) — and often transactions do not come to the attention of the taxman; hence the term 'black economy' to apply to this area which is considered morally suspect.

PROSPECTS

A helpful suggestion about the emerging structure of economic activity, involving the informal as well as the formal economy, was recently put forward by a joint European/North American task force of business thinkers. It has been summarised as follows:*

> New production technologies, including information technologies and the micro-processor, are likely to lead to more highly automated, more capital-intensive mass production processes. They could also lead to more decentralised living and working. They will probably do both. As a result, a four-sectoral economic structure may emerge in the industrialised countries in the 1980s on the following lines:
> Sector A: a capital-intensive, highly automated and highly productive sector, including big manufacturing industries and big commercial services like airlines, international banking, and telecommunications;
> Sector B: a labour-intensive, large-scale, service sector, including services like education and health;
> Sector C: a revived small-scale, entrepreneurial, local sector, consisting of a very wide range of industrial, commercial and non-profit enterprises (the latter including community enterprises, common ownerships, work

* From *The Redistribution of Work*, James Robertson, Turning Point Paper No. 1.

66

experience projects, voluntary groups, amenity groups and other socio-economic activities), and supported by new locally based institutions such as local enterprise trusts;

Sector D: a revived household and neighbourhood sector, in which work is generally informal and unpaid and marginally paid, often takes the form of DIY or self-help, and is often difficult to distinguish from leisure.

Sectors A and B are entirely in the 'formal economy', and in general are likely to provide more and more limited and specialised job opportunities. Sectors C and D merge into the informal economy, in which very substantial growth is already taking place,* and will continue to do so.

We can expect a revival of local economies (including the small firms sector), with more use of local resources to meet local needs, thus reducing energy costs and improving both the quality and the quantity of work. There should also be growth in community enterprise projects, youth opportunities projects, work experience projects, local amenity projects, training projects and various kinds of voluntary service projects, on lines begun in recent years by the Manpower Services Commission, local authorities, charitable organisations, voluntary services and other non-profit concerns. These will become a permanent feature and it will be accepted that young people should be given opportunities for community service, as has recently been proposed.

More than anything we can foresee a substantial development of the household economy. Miniaturised technology in many fields (including microprocessors, micro-computers and video terminals) is making it possible to do at home work now done in factories and offices. People who handle information, like computer programmers and insurance salespeople, are moving in this direction already.

* See for example *Can I Have it in Cash?* edited by Stuart Henry, Astrological Books, London, 1981.

Increasing numbers of people are spending more time on DIY and other informal kinds of work for themselves, their families, and their friends and neighbours — including food growing, car maintenance, plumbing, electrical work, carpentry and various aspects of home maintenance. Arrangements for exchanging skills and services with neighbours outside the formal labour market are spreading.

Since most people still identify the limited jobs in the formal economy with work, and since (unless we reorganise things) they are the main cash points, then all kinds of sharing arrangements must be promoted. These include early retirement — leading to a change in the meaning of retirement, which could become for many people a system of accumulating sufficient credits in the formal economy to release their energies for more real, more freely chosen work. It could also include a reduction in hours and flexible time arrangements (a thousand-hour year is being promoted), part-time employment, and job-sharing. All this will tend to increase activity in the informal sector, as it becomes commonly understood that 'formal' work is only a *part* of a working life.

But what of the so-called 'black economy'? How do we cope with this morally ambiguous area of cash payments which evade both the taxman and the social security system?

THE INTERFACE PROBLEM

The problem of the 'black economy' is an interface problem; it occurs at the interface between the formal and the informal economies, and it is the consequence of the way in which we think about these two spheres. We can of course tidy up and tighten up the rules; but in order to get the problem in perspective we now need to think more deeply about the nature of the 'two economies' which cause the interface problem.

We have already said that the informal economy is as big and as important as the formal economy; but this is not enough. The informal economy and the formal economy are not the same kind of thing at all. The informal economy is the ordinary process of living, helping, sharing, growing, exchanging. You cannot draw lines within it and say 'here the informal economy stops'. It is the everyday process of living in society. Having friends round to supper could be seen as part of the informal economy — and for that matter so could a mother breast-feeding her child.

The informal economy exists before the formal economy. There are still simpler societies in the world which have no formal economy at all.

It is an abstraction from the mass of human activity which we have called economic; it is simply that part of it for which tokens are useful. It is not therefore another 'kind' of economy; it is a part of the economy viewed from a specific and limited point of view.

What has happened in industrial society is that the process of industrialisation and commercialisation resulted in the 'token' bit of the economy becoming so dominant that people forgot its origins — and in a sense forgot themselves. This had the result of debasing the meaning of work. It became entirely quantified and 'alienated'. Instead of being the self-directed transforming activity, by which we co-operatively mould the environment and satisfy our material and spiritual needs, work came to mean for most people turning up with an anonymous crowd to look after someone else's machine for someone else's material gain, and to have a fractional role in producing something which in no sense expressed, or belonged to, or was even used by the person who made it.

What went wrong with the way we think about our lives is that we came to think of the token system as the 'real' economy and the rest as somehow insubstantial. Life is the basic non-money value on which all other real values are based — like health, creativity,

69

fun, friendship — and work. Everyone knows that his own life does not have 'a price'. No-one in his senses would accept any sum of money if the condition was that he would immediately be shot! If life cannot be costed then a part of it cannot be costed either. Work cannot be just 'a commodity'; we may have to 'sell it'; but it is also part of our lives, and therefore not for sale! — any more than the whole of our life is for sale. If all our lives we ticked like taxi-meters we should be no more human than a taxi; if our living and loving were charged for then suicide would be the only possible conclusion, for nothing is more uneconomic than staying alive.

The industrial and commercial system has brought immense benefit to us, and it will continue to do so. It is simply a question of making sure it is properly rooted in real living which cannot be either objectified or costed.

So what about the 'interface' problem between the 'formal' and 'informal' economy? The government has to collect taxes, and pay benefits, and therefore have a firm base on which to calculate people's participation in the formal economy; and since the formal bit merges in a messy way with informal, the edges are bound to be ragged. One possible strategy for coping with this interface problem is to extend management, measurement and control systems further and further into the informal sector. Thus there could be a much closer control on casual payments for casual jobs, with severer penalties for concealment; there could be an attempt to supervise and quantify bartering and exchange arrangements, and even self-help.

But where would you draw the line? If we try to manage, measure and control the informal exchange of goods and services, what about people helping each other in general — supporting each other in need — loving each other, for that matter, which is a rather important 'service'? The fact is that the informal economy is not *difficult* to manage, measure or control; it is in principle impossible to manage, measure and control. If, in spite of this, the government or any other agencies seek to extend the control system into the heartland of human society, the results are unsatisfactory all round. For those who seek to control, the results are exasperating, leading inevitably towards ever increasing control and ever increasing efficiency; and for those who are victims of the control, the effect is increasingly to undermine the fundamental liberties which alone give meaning to life. For society as a whole, the attempt to generalise the control and measurement model at a political level is profoundly corrupting, because it poisons the understanding of what it means to be a person, and how this differs from being a thing; and it is only as persons that we are the bearers of human rights.

This presents government with a very difficult problem. We say to government, which conceives itself as a vast management system, that there is a whole 10/11ths of the iceberg of society that is in principle unmanageable. How on earth can they manage the little bit at the top if the rest is totally unmanageable — and in any case how on earth can they draw a line between the manageable bit and the unmanageable bit?

Yet this need not present so great a problem when thinking about the functions of government after all; because the job of government is not to manage society — or even to manage the economy. The function of government is to maintain human rights, the foundation of which is freedom and self-determinnation.

A SOCIAL WAGE

There is no doubt whatsoever that the greatest disservice which the present system does to the informal sector is to provide a social benefit system for the unemployed which is reduced in line with earnings. On the one hand you can be totally supported by the state, on the other hand you can earn a full wage; but in between, in the grey area of low-paid work, casual work, part-time work, semi-voluntary work, you either cheat or lose most of what you earn since all earnings above a minimum allowance are deducted from benefits. The government in this way imposes in effect 100% tax on small earnings; and this must inevitably appear as a *penalty* for working.

There is no shortage whatsoever of work in society, even if we define work in the narrow sense of jobs for which somebody will pay something; but many of these remain undone in a society screaming out for jobs because they are in the 'grey' area, between total social security and full wages, where society through the political system has created a Slough of Despond called Cheat-or-Lose. Yet practically all chances of vitality and growth lie precisely in the grey area. Most jobs which people make for themselves grow from seeds like plants; they don't spring out of the earth ready made. As long as this is seen as an interface problem, it cannot be completely resolved. If the state provides just for the unemployed, then it must arrange phased reductions as earnings begin to come in, thus imposing an apparently penalising tax in the crossover phase.

With this difficulty in mind, it is essential now to look again at a proposal which eliminates this partic-ular interface problem by radically rethinking and simplifying the government's role. The proposal is for a basic Social Wage. The essential idea of a Social Wage is that every person receives a tax free payment sufficient to maintain an acceptable standard of living. This payment is unconditional; as long as you are human, you get it. All other incomes, other than the social wage, are subject to taxation. Such a system would automatically replace the whole of the national insurance benefit system, a host of means-tested benefits, and all personal allowances under income tax.

72

The social wage would clarify the role of government and distinguish it clearly from the role of the job market. The role of the government acting as a community agency, is to pay the social wage and thus ensure that no-one is deprived of basic necessities. The function of the market can then in principle be entirely separated from the problem of basic necessities; it can become a free market system in which any bargain can be made which suits both sides — including of course both very low and very high payments for full-time or part-time permanent or temporary employment.

The scheme would have to be paid for out of the taxation system. The basic principle is simple; though the details of tax options is complex. The money paid in the social wage would be received from personal tax, by virtue of abolishing personal allowances and raising the basic tax rate by the required amount. **The actual change in money received by the average wage earner would be quite small** — only the theory would have changed dramatically; it is important to remember this when calculating the *cost* of the social wage, which has been dismissed up to now as 'astronomical'. If the social wage costs me £4,000. and I receive £4,000, it costs me nothing. In theory, it should be possible just to *rethink* the present system without changing anyone's income; in reality, however, low earners would be better off, and some of those earning large incomes would be worse off, because their increase in taxation would be greater than their social wage.*

It should also be borne in mind however, that there will be a very strong case, as society evolves in the direction of a few high production and low employment 'cash points', for recovery of much of the social

* The taxation implications of a 'full social dividend' were discussed briefly in the Report of the Meade Committee, *The Structure and Reform of Direct Taxation*, (Allen & Unwin 1978), pp. 271-4, on the assumption that the social dividend was fixed at 40% of average earnings taxation, and that a standard taxation rate of 55% is imposed to cover this.

wage from these centres through appropriate company taxation thus reducing the extra burden of personal taxation on high wage earners.

The advantages of the social wage over the present system are considerable. First of all, it is a system which is very easy to understand and very easy to administer; and it is one of the essential principles of good government to make rules which are simple and easy to administer. Not only is this important because clear rules create security and harmony; it is also important because it saves a great deal of money. The complex administration needed for the present system of taxation and benefits is very expensive. In fact, it must be admitted that one problem of the social wage is that it would lead to large scale unemployment of civil servants! Secondly, this system would be highly effective in eliminating poverty by guaranteeing a minimum income. The present system is of course in theory designed to eliminate poverty, since everyone is in theory entitled to receive an amount at least to the level of supplementary benefit. In fact there is a great deal of poverty, due partly to the inadequacy of the benefit system and partly to the failure to take up benefits because of their complexity and because of the stigma which is attached to them. The social wage would overcome all these difficulties. Its level would be openly and publicly negotiated, and would be unlikely to fall below what was needed for decent living; and everyone would take it up, because it would be very easy to do so; and because everyone was entitled there would be no stigma attached.

Much more important than either of these would be the enormous release in energy, which would result from eliminating the Slough of Cheat-or-Lose. Under the old system, what you earn you lose; under the new, whatever you earn would be of benefit to you — though justly taxed. Perhaps a few people would not work at all. However, if work is a fundamental

74

need, the number of idlers will be small — certainly less than under the present system, where there is a strong dis-incentive to work.* It would be quite open to anyone to work either for himself or for someone else at a low rate of pay, knowing that even the low rate of pay was worth something. It is probably that as a result of cheap labour contracts at the bottom and most 'informal' end of the market, labour costs in general would over a period of years be substantially reduced; and this in turn would lead to substantial re-employment in the more formal sectors of the economy. All this paid work which would otherwise be left undone would of course benefit the formal economy, and generate taxes to pay the social wage.

Apart from being much simpler, how would such a system relate to what happens now? In fact the Social Wage scheme is very much in line with a direction of advance not only in Britain, but in most industrialised societies.

The acceptance of a basic supplementary benefit level already means that there is a minimum wage guarantee accepted by the community. Unconditional and untaxed child benefits imply an acceptance of a 'social wage' for children; unconditional old age pensions are an acceptance of a social wage for the old (though in both cases the levels are inadequate). The main difference between the social wage and the present system is that some benefits for the unem-ployed are conditional on being available for work; but in many districts this condition is also a mere formality, and in some cases, as for instance where useful volunteer work is being done, the requirement of availability is widely disregarded.

The fact that many of our present arrangements *point towards* a social wage means that it is possible

* Repeated surveys in many countries all show that the vast majority of people, even among hard-core unemployed, say that they would want to work even if it were not an economic necessity. See *Work Employment and Unemployment*, Marie Jahoda and Howard Rush, Science Policy Research Unit, University of Sussex, Brighton (1980).

to adopt a 'gradualist' approach to this question. In April 1981, Sir George Young (Parliamentary Under-Secretary, Health and Social Security) announced that the earnings limit for people receiving unemployment benefit was to be increased from 75p to £2 a day; and that voluntary organisations were to be able to recruit unemployed people as full-time employees for up to twelve months to help unemployed people to find suitable work. These are small steps; but they are small steps which make a lot of sense when the general principle and goal is understood and accepted.

There is also another way of looking at the present arrangements. The community already provides to everyone a substantial unconditional benefit in the form of education, social services, roads, fire services, etc. No-one has to prove that he 'deserves' these; and they constitute a very substantial social wage in kind.

Most industrialised countries have accepted in practice this basic approach; and the tendency is for the basic guaranteed living wage to rise as a percentage of average income. What is needed therefore is a conceptual leap forward which will enable us to re-interpret the situation, discard the rubbish and open up new avenues of exploration. It is very much like the situation in which science finds itself when an old hypothesis is collapsing under pressure of conflicting evidence — like Ptolemy's astronomy, based on the idea that the earth was in the centre. The temptation is to multiply hypotheses and try to fit them all together, so that you produce more and more confused and complicated diagrams. The creative leap produces a new and much simpler hypothesis, like imagining the sun in the centre, and opens new perspectives for research.

The change of thinking involved is not just to do with money incentives. The financial structure is a symbol; it carries a meaning which relates in a healthy society to the underlying values of life. With a social wage not only would financial incentive systems
76

change, but so would the meaning which the financial system embodies.

It could be argued that the change of meaning would be a bad one. It would simply reinforce the image of the 'providing state'. However there are very important differences between providing money unconditionally as a guaranteed social wage and providing goods and services. The first difference is that providing money is providing resources and choice, and therefore enhancing freedom. The second is that the simple and unconditional provision of money through the social wage could be administered with a minimum of bureaucracy — indeed it could be administered *automatically* without any bureaucracy at all. There is no reason why with modern computer technology, there should not be an account for every person in the country to which an appropriate amount is automatically credited. This would minimise the danger of bureaucratic centralism; and it would make clear that this is a community self-regulating system, based on commonly agreed principles of justice.

The positive meaning embodied in the social wage would be that of human rights. Just as we agree that a person has a right to life, and that this right is unconditional, so we would say as a community through the social wage that everyone has an unconditional right to the means necessary to sustain life in a fully human sense.

If this is what society would mean by the social wage for the individual, the meaning of work would be correspondingly transformed. 'Sweated labour' or 'exploitation' would lose their meaning. Without the social wage, it is possible to think that a wage 'bought' a part of a person's life; that it is therefore an estimate of what he is worth. But when a social wage is paid, no-one is buying anyone else's life, or a part of it; people are making free contractual arrangements with each other, arrangements which have no implication about his value as a person. His value as a person is expressed in the language of human rights, and incorporated in the social wage which guarantees them.

With the decline of the need to work simply to remain 'afloat', the other motivations which we know to underlie work would rise to the surface — creativity, social recognition, development of skills and talents; service to others, self-realisation — precisely those motivations which in fact already impel all those who 'make the running' in society, whether industrialists, artists or politicians.

A new kind of work ethic and a new educational system would be called for; the drives involved are powerful, and far from producing a generation of loafers, would release energy and creativity at present deadened by much meaningless employment which masquerades as work.

Chapter Five
HOUSING: PROBLEMS

The right to work is much in the news, and will remain a major concern of government for the rest of this century. Equally basic to human needs is the right to a home. Like the right to work, it is closely bound up with one's identity as a human being. In this chapter we shall consider the responsibility of a human rights-orientated government in this field.

THE RIGHT TO A HOME

The right to a home or to 'living space' has been proclaimed by most modern governments, including our own, as a basis for political action, and to that extent promoting this right could be considered part of the 'custom and practice of civilised nations'. It is not a right which is spelt out in the Universal Declaration of Human Rights, or in the Covenants based on them; but it is implied in other rights which are spelt out, in particular in rights relating to the family and to privacy. Article 12 of the Declaration for instance states that

> No-one shall be subjected to arbitrary interference with his privacy, family, home or correspondence . . . everyone has a right to the protection of the law against such interference or attack.

79

It is common sense that if a person has a right to live, he must have a right to space to live in; and clearly this space must be more than a man-sized box. How should this right be interpreted as the basis for a political programme?

The right to living space has at its core the right to home-space — to a personal or family 'habitat'. A habitat is a habitual living space — a space where you normally eat, sleep, work and play; but having the right normally to eat, sleep, work and play in a place is not sufficient to make it a home. The ordinary commercial system provides for people with money to buy space for all these activities, like restaurants, hotels, and sports centres — but these spaces are not home, or bits of homes, even if they are habitually used.

At a deeper level, home implies a certain intimate relationship between oneself and a particular part of the world — the personal or family 'habitat'. It is such a radical relationship that it is difficult to translate into other terms; It is closely connected with the experience of having a physical body; it is in a sense an extension of the physical body, like clothes. That is why the physical boundaries of the home are so important, and why rituals of entry and departure are required in all cultures. It is why burglary has such a profoundly unsettling effect, especially on women.*

Like the physical body, the home is also an expression of the individual or group to which it belongs. It is both their 'face' presented to the world, and the material for their own self-realisation. Home-making is an activity shared by all human societies, and for that matter the biological basis of it can be seen in animal society also. Nomadic groups even more than

* Richard Leakey in a recent TV series, *The Making of Mankind*, said "Animals mark off territory, some apes or monkeys return to their favourite trees or cliffs, but only humans create a temporary or permanent base — a home; a place where men, women and children return after a day spent collecting food; where the very young, the old and the sick can be cared for."

settled groups have rituals to define home space and the rights associated with it; and the gipsy's caravan is no less sacred because it moves relatively to the outside world. From the gipsy child's point of view, it is the rest of the world that moves, and the caravan that is stable; just as from all our points of view our own bodies are the constant reference points from which we relate to a changing world.

From the perception of what a 'home' is, certain rules emerge about home space which have wide validity.

First of all, home space must be secure from intrusion (hence the wording of Article 12 of the United Nations Declaration). There must be a maximum degree of control over who comes and who goes. Hospitality enriches home space; but invasion desecrates it. The more there is intrusion, the less there is a home.

Secondly, because home is the expression and the self realisation of those dwelling within it, there must be a maximum degree of freedom from constraint, and freedom to construct and create within the home space.

The less there is control of living space, the less there is a home. Beyond the inner core of home space, there are other categories of living space which are important. I discussed earlier the dwindling of the household economy, and of the likely revival of this economy in the future. We are living therefore at a time when the common meaning of the word 'home' is at a low ebb; it has become possible to think of it as no more than a roosting box from which a daily flight into 'the economy' originates.

In longer-term historical perspective, and in terms of basic human needs, it is important to have a wider view. We must therefore include in the right to living space a right to working space, or alternatively to support space — space in which to engage in work on a small-scale either for the household economy or for the wider economy. This clearly includes in our society garden space and workshop space, in the same way that it includes kitchen space.

Outside these rights to home space and work space, there are other rights to living space of a less exclusive kind, but equally demanding of respect. High in priority is a right to recreation space or play space for adults and for children — a right which should include wide-ranging privileges of access, where such access does not conflict with more fundamental rights.

To whom does the right of living-space belong? To individuals, families or communities? Something like the family unit is the most usual subject of the right to living-space in our society, as it was in pre-Norman times, but clearly individuals and larger groups must not be excluded. Some people choose to live alone; others choose to live in groups, like members of religious orders or community groups. The kind of living-space required by the individual, family and community differs; but the right to space must be equally respected.

Since the right to living space is a fundamental human right, it is the government's job to maintain and promote this right. Before we consider how best to do this job in the context of present day Britain, we need first of all to look at existing systems and see how they are functioning.

THE PRESENT SYSTEM AND ITS PROBLEMS

Within the housing system in the U.K. there are two major sub-systems — owner-occupation and council tenancy. In addition there are a number of minor systems, including private rental.

Government involvement in these systems is enormous; and so also are the problems. Present figures suggest, if there is no dramatic change in policy, that Council house waiting lists of 1.2 million will rise to 2 million, with a waiting time for the average family of 21.4 years. The crude figures conceal a human reality which is a nightmare for thousands of families. In many hostels for the homeless up and down the country families live in incredibly sordid conditions over which they exercise no control whatsoever. *The Sunday Times* (8 February 1981) carried an article about a typical family of eight children living in a room 20′ x 10′ beset by the clamour of traffic, cries of babies through partition walls, and the stink of urine from neglected lavatories.

According to government statistics there are 1½ million people 'officially' homeless, in the sense that they are in temporary accommodation provided by local authorities for homeless people; and this must be just the tip of an iceberg, because for every person who gets temporary accommodation there must be many who conceal their real need or find some other makeshift.

The groups of people who are particularly deprived include immigrants and other recent arrivals, transients or people who cannot become permanently settled, including students, young people, single or married, who are trying to set up home for the first time, and low-paid households who are poor by any standards — notably large families, single-parent families, the chronic sick, the unemployed and pensioners.

Clearly there is a problem here. Human rights are not being maintained, and government is failing in a fundamental duty.

In order to focus more clearly on the problem however, we need to look at two major housing sub-systems in turn, and see how they are functioning and how they are failing.

Those in owner-occupied housing have the maximum control over their living space. They are the most content, and would agree that their rights have been most fully met. However, because of the rising prices of houses for sale, it is becoming increasingly difficult for people who do not already own houses to climb on the band wagon. Those who were lucky enough to buy houses in the mid-1960s or earlier have benefited from an enormous gain in capital value — in many cases they have houses worth four or five times what they paid for them, and if they have an outstanding mortgage it is only a small one based on the original price. But new prospective house-buyers are faced with having to borrow five times as much and at a much higher rate of interest.

This is not just a difficulty for many people, it is an impossibility. Most Building Societies will only lend 2½ times the householder's annual income. This means that in many districts a large section of the population (those whose incomes are less than one third the price of a house) are not able to borrow enough to buy. As for the large and increasing army of unemployed, they are of course totally excluded from the housing market.

In the field of council housing, there are long waiting lists. But even for the lucky ones who are 'housed' in council housing, there are serious problems of a kind which do not afflict owner-occupiers.

The name 'Council Housing' is loaded with over-tones for all of us — whether we are Council tenants or not; and these overtones are generally speaking bad ones. Council housing developed at the end of the nineteenth century as housing for the poor, organised by a paternalistic local authority; legislation described it specifically as 'Housing for the Working Classes'. With the growth of the public housing system, a trad-ition of bureaucracy has developed which traps both tenants and administrators.

Many authorities for instance 'classify' tenants according to 'standards' of cleanliness, family life, etc., and allocate houses accordingly. Inevitably this means having teams of inspectors who work under various disguises; it means secret lists, and it means that some areas are 'dustbin districts' for undesirables. Some assume a right to evict tenants for transgressing rules of behaviour (like keeping pets for instance). A

84

recent scandal in Burnham (Bucks) relates to a local authority which refuses to let a man cut his own grass! Given a large bureaucracy administering these rules, with no procedure of appeal or complaint against the housing authority, injustices can and do occur — with the local authority acting as judge, jury, prosecutor and executioner.

On the tenants side, the problem of entrenched attitudes is just as bad. Common attitudes among council tenants (not universal of course) are 'unneighbourliness, often resulting in loneliness, and an acceptance of the notion that people in council houses have failed, have not quite made it; this is frequently expressed as a frustrated desire to buy a house off the estate.'* Worst of all is the attitude of dependence and frustration which becomes worse as the shortage of houses becomes more acute, and the power of the administration grows.

The problem of attitudes is reflected in the state of the buildings. There are council estates in the country where standards of maintenance are high; but in general, there is an enormous problem of residential decay in council estates all over the country. Tenants are rarely allowed to make any structural alterations without obtaining written permission, and in many cases not even to decorate. Repairs and maintenance are normally the responsibility of the local authority, and as the authorities increase in size the logistical task of organising an army of maintenance men becomes horrific.† Problems associated with condensation, flat roofs, and flaking concrete cladding are proving unmanageable. The collapse of the Ronan Point tower block was a prophetic event; in Birkenhead, the local authority has adopted the final solution of demolition for two blocks of maisonettes built in

* *Tenants Take-Over*, Colin Ward, Architectural Press 1975, p. 23.
† In Camden alone 450 men are employed in day to day maintenance of 22,000 homes, trying to cope with 42,000 orders for items such as broken windows, cracked basins, and leaking pipes.

1957, and in the 1980s such demolition will inevitably become a common public spectacle.

As a result of the decay of council property and problems of vandalism a substantial proportion of council houses remain empty in spite of the pressing needs of the homeless.

PURCHASE AND PROVISION: GOVERNMENT POLICY IN PERSPECTIVE

Distribution of Housing Systems

	1914	1947	1964	1974
Owner Occupiers	9%	26%	44%	53%
Council tenants	1	13	26	33
Private rental and others	90	61	30	14

Government involvement in housing, which has a long history, has clearly been motivated by a concern for human rights, and a genuine acceptance of responsibility for the homeless. This action has not on the whole been successful, and we are now entering a phase when the state of homelessness will constitute an indictment of the policy of any government which does not have a well thought out remedy. A brief historical perspective will help to show how well-motivated government action has turned out to be largely counter-productive.

The majority of ordinary people until quite recent times took it as a matter of course that they were responsible for the building of their own houses, whether they used their own labour or that of friends and tradesmen. On the Island of Lewis, the houses or 'clachans' are still built entirely by the peasants themselves, and there are no craftsmen who devote their whole time to building.

The big change in the organisation of building came in the eighteenth and nineteenth centuries when we changed from being a small agricultural nation living in the country to a large industrial nation living in towns. As the population rose in leaps and bounds, and vast numbers, excluded from the land by enclosures, crowded into the cities to find 'employment' in the factories and the mines, it became clear that traditional methods of building and the self-help techniques of the countryside were no longer adequate.

The new urban poor had to be housed, and in a hurry. The first and by far the largest response to this need was that housing itself became another large commercial concern, an adjunct of the factory system. The industrialists had to house their workers, and they put up the maximum number of minimum sized houses as close to the factory as possible, producing the typical industrial slums that we can still see in parts of England.

The speculative private landlord also flourished, and through the eighteenth and nineteenth centuries it was the private landlord who provided the greater part of housing in the towns and cities. It was good business. People had to live somewhere, and if you could supply the small amount of capital needed to build you could get a very good and secure return on rents for an indefinite period. There was no longer any social or cultural tie between landlord and tenant — it was an unregulated commercial arrangement, and in general the private landlord would cram as many people into a small space with as few amenities as possible and charge whatever rental could be extracted.

The result of private enterprise industrial housing was the most appalling living conditions ever experienced in the history of our civilisation. It is this kind of development that produced eventually the counter-development of government building and planning.

Local authority action began with an order to safeguard the public health; action fully justifiable on the grounds of a right to a safe environment. Rules were made to reduce crowding and control disease. Pressures on the private landlord gradually increased, and the powers of the local authority also increased. Eventually, the Local Authorities were given power in 1890 in the Housing and Working Classes Act to *provide* new homes for the 'labouring classes'.

During the 1914-18 war, as a result of public outrage when servicemen's wives were evicted for non-payment of rent, the Rent Acts were passed to freeze rents for the duration of the war. This resulted in a further decline in the supply of privately rented property. After the war, the government began to build 'Homes for Heroes', and between the two wars about a million 'Council Houses' were built by local authorities. The Second World War gave a similar but much more powerful boost to municipal housing — more homes were needed for even more heroes. State action was taken for granted, and the identification of socialism with State provision was widely accepted. There was then a surge of Council building during the 1950s and 1960s (including tower-blocks) coupled with massive programmes of slum clearance, and it was during this period that the shape of the present housing situation began to emerge.

Private rental declined steadily during this period as government constriction of the private landlord gathered pace, and other forms of investment became more attractive. Owner-occupation on the other hand grew rapidly, thanks largely to the development of Building Societies.

The role of the local authority in planning increased in parallel with its role of supervising and constructing houses. The sprawling and ugly growth of towns between wars and the social disorder associated with the depression led to more and more demand for central government controls, and by the end of the

Second World War the stage was set for the New Towns Act and the Town and Country Planning Act, which set up the basic machinery for state control and initiation of development, to which we are now accustomed.

Looking back over the history of government involvement in housing, we can now see how it began in a small way with regulations necessary to protect people's basic rights, whether to health, security of tenure, or a clean environment; how these regulations have gradually accumulated into a massive system that increasingly hinders the normal functioning of the community, whether through self-help or through the market; and how regulations have led by gradual stages to provision, first on a small scale and then on the massive scale to which we have grown accustomed.

Chapter Six
HOUSING: STRATEGIES

With the wisdom of hindsight we can now begin to see what has gone wrong with government policies in the housing field.

The underlying error is to identify the right to a home with the provision of houses. Government provision divides society into 'providers' and those provided for, and tends both to perpetuate itself in time and to increase in volume; it undermines the element of self-determination which gives meaning to this as to other human rights.

Combining provision with large-scale organisation compounds the difficulties; the circle of accountability is too large. The individual ratepayer and taxpayer 'purchases' an undefinable bit of everybody else's house through a massive and complex bureaucracy which is impossible to understand or control. Separating people from responsibility for either the creation or management of their homes results in wastage of resources; and *it is from these wasted resources that the homes which are needed could be created.*

The most obvious wastage is in land, the most fundamental physical resource. Large systems cannot focus on or use economically small parcels of land. Consequently large areas of countryside are used up by housing estates, when there is ample unused space within existing urban areas, usually in small irregular plots.*

Less obvious, but even more important, is the wastage of human resources — people's own creativity, skill and ingenuity. Many frustrated and unemployed families in decaying high-rise flats could, in a different system, be pouring endless energy, dedication and skill into organising or even constructing their own living environment.

Closely connected with the wastage incurred by lost and neglected opportunities and resources is the positive wastage of large sums of public money by inappropriate house provision. Of course local authorities vary greatly in their performance. But in general, large-scale planning and house construction projects throughout the world result in a coarse system which fails to match the fine grain of human needs,† leading frequently to early dereliction and dilapidation.

The mistake of large-scale provision for an intensely personal need is compounded by a mistake about public purchasing. Public purchasing, as we have seen, is appropriate when the benefit of what is purchased is communal and not individual. There is no case in general for the public purchase of homes the benefit of which is clearly to individuals. But even assuming that a local authority has a rightfully delegated task of purchasing houses for the community, it is inappropriate that the local authority should purchase from itself. The house buying bureaucracy is incestuously bound to a house planning bureaucracy, and the offspring are frequently monstrous and sometimes short-lived.

---

* A survey of vacant plots in New Ham carried out by students of the the Architectural Association revealed sites for an estimated 4,000 dwellings, declared unusable by the local authority because of their smallness and irregular sizes.

† Certain council flats in Camden, (built at a cost to the public of over £70,000 per unit), have oil-fired central heating incorporated in the walls which individuals cannot adjust or turn off.

GOVERNMENT AS ENABLER

As a home is the most highly individualised possession we ever have, individual and local control and responsibility is of prime importance; and private ownership is the most complete and individual form of control and responsibility which we have. However, it is important not to see private ownership as a kind of absolute, and other forms of control as being irrelevant. Private ownership is just a certain package of legal rights in relation to property — rights which are properly limited by just rules of the game established by government, such as legitimate planning controls. There are also other packages of rights to property, graduated in the degree of control and responsibility they confer.

All these packages of rights are normally acquired and exchanged through the market. The present 'housing market' includes the *whole system* through which the rights over home space are purchased and exchanged; it includes therefore private rental and local authority housing as well as private housing. The public housing sub-system is a mixture of communal purchasing and private purchasing (through rents), and cannot be separated from the rest of the market.

How does present government activity relate to the market in this broad sense?

CLOGGING UP THE MARKET

The private rental sector of the housing market has declined to a point where it now only provides 10% of the homes. Yet there is a very large demand for private rental, and a very large untapped supply in the form of unoccupied or under-occupied premises. The decline of the private rental sector is in a large measure due to government intervention. Through rent control, security of tenure government has tried to secure justice for tenants; but as a result, a great many rooms and houses stand empty throughout the country, simply because their owners are afraid that if they have tenants they will never be able to get them out.

The public rental and private home-ownership sector of the housing market are also impeded by government activity. Everything, somehow or another, is subsidised. Council housing is heavily subsidised — in the case of new housing often to the extent of 80% of the cost, and private housing is subsidised by the granting of income tax relief.

Subsidies of an undefined and generalised nature are in general more a way of clogging up the market system than of oiling it. The motivation for these subsidies is to help people to acquire homes. Through the subsidy system we all purchase communally an undefinable bit of everyone else's house. There is however no logic about the subsidies, and very little accountability. Council house subsidies are still based on an inappropriate idea of provision for the poor or the working class, and perpetuates outmoded stereotypes; and the tax exemption for home-owners is equally without any obvious basis in justice.

The existing subsidy system is not sufficiently radical to guarantee the right to a house, but is sufficient to obstruct the market system, damage the supply of houses, and because of the confused association with justice and equality it causes bitterness and recrimination between conflicting groups who consider they are not receiving their due.

OILING THE MARKET

If subsidies were gradually removed, and progress was made at the same time towards an effective social wage or minimum income guarantee, the market would function better to meet people's needs. Houses would be more fully used, and many of the now vacant premises would be occupied; the supply of houses would increase, and prices would fall.

In the meantime, there are many good and discriminating ways in which the government can oil the housing market. Some provisions of this kind were included in the 1980 Housing Bill. Local authorities and the Housing Corporation were empowered and encouraged by this Bill to guarantee loans from Building Societies to individuals or groups who would not secure loans without such a guarantee — such as self-build groups. Local authorities were also encouraged to enter into equity-sharing schemes, in which part of a house is publicly purchased and rented and part is privately bought — thus enabling a low income family to enter the market, and progressively to increase his share.

'Homesteading' is another promising scheme pioneered in this country by the GLC. This is a way of enabling people with small resources to restore for themselves derelict housing, which they then own. The GLC identifies suitable houses, advertises the scheme, and offers mortgages to suitable applicants to include the cost of self-help repairs and renovation.

The sale of council houses is another important strand in a multiple strategy. It is clear from the limited experience in this country, and extensive experience in other European countries, that the attitude of council tenants to property is transformed when they become house-owners. The amount of care and attention and energy that is devoted without any pressure from above to maintaining, improving and extending the property for which owners feel responsible is something far beyond anything that could be achieved by spending more and more government money on building up a bigger and better system of centralised 'servicing'.

Selling off council housing however only makes sense as part of a general policy to maintain the right to a home. If in a specific situation privatisation leads directly to homelessness, it cannot be the right policy at that time.

Part of the problem is that, due to the decline in

private rental housing, Council housing is now virtually the sole source of rentable property in many districts. Clearly there is and always will be a widespread need for rented accommodation, especially for people who are only temporarily in a certain district or who do not have the capital to buy, or who choose to use what capital they have in another way. Renting is an option which it is essential to retain, and which is especially important for those who are at risk of finding themselves without a home at all. This need is at the root of the present conflict about 'selling off' council houses.

It is however a mistake to assume that the need for rented accommodation must be met by government provision. Already some tentative steps have been taken towards 'loosening up' the private rental market by introducing 'shorthold tenure'. Much more important is the introduction in the 1980 Housing Act of 'assured tenancies' — which simply means that registered institutions will be able to charge economic Rents. The Abbey National Building Society has taken the lead by setting up the Abbey Housing Association, which was the first to register under the act. The Abbey Housing Association* will now be able to build houses for rent, using money invested in the Abbey National Building Society.

The entry of the Building Societies into the private rental field is potentially of great significance for loosening up the system. The service performed by Building Societies for owner-occupation could be extended to regenerate the private rental sector. The government could then play its legitimate role as enabler — responsible for registering societies and safeguarding standards, but otherwise leaving the market free to operate.

* Current legislation prevents Building Societies from *building* houses; therefore a new entity, the Abbey Housing Association had to be formed.

LOCALISATION AND PERSONALISATION OF CONTROL AND RESPONSIBILITY

The future of the large public housing sector in the country is a major problem. There are packages of rights over council houses short of private ownership which can be more appropriate in some cases, and can be an important move towards responsibility and control. It is an important principle to begin where you are; and at present many millions depend on public housing and are realising their right to home space to some extent through this system. As with employment, we have had to live for some time with systems we would not have chosen if we started from scratch; but to abandon them abruptly can be an assault on human rights, even if the motives for abandonment are good.

Localisation and personalisation of control and responsibility should be a guiding principle in this sector as elsewhere. The 'Tenant's Charter', embodied in the 1980 Housing Act, strengthens rights to security of tenure, and to carrying out improvements. 'Mobility schemes', pioneered in the London area, enable people to take their own initiatives to exchange houses within the council system. These are all ways of strengthening the package of 'rights' which constitute the right to a home.

There is also scope for co-operative arrangements. A good example is in Oslo, where a municipal estate was transferred over a period of years from the ownership of the local authority to associations of tenants. The initiative came from the local authority, not from the tenants; and the reason for that was that the estate was a big headache to housing managers — low standards, resistance to rent increases, run-down appearance. A series of meetings arranged by the housing manager led to the acceptance by tenants of co-operative ownership. Today the estate is transformed. The members have cared for their own property, and have ensured that others have done so; and they charge themselves 'fees for occupation' higher than the rents against which they protested. Co-owners feel very strongly that the great advantage of the scheme is security of tenure. Other advantages rated highly by occupants are having a say about their surroundings, living in a friendly community, and living in an orderly well-managed estate.

Localising responsibility and oiling the market by appropriate legislation is one aspect of the government's function in relation to housing. There is another function however of quite a different kind because it relates to different kind of resources; and that is the function of trusteeship in relation to the land.

GOVERNMENT AS TRUSTEE OF LAND

Land is the basis of everyone's living space, but it is not a 'commodity'. It is something quite different from any other 'property' that man lays claim to. In the words of Mark Twain, 'Nobody's making it any more'!

There is something absurd about claiming in regard to land the same kind of property rights that are claimed for other things that can be produced, destroyed, consumed. Most civilisations, including ours at an earlier stage, have a strongly religious attitude to the division and use of land, since it is seen to be not just a commodity but the very basis of life itself — like the water we drink and the air we breathe — and therefore something closely related to a god who is the source of life, and the concern of the community as a whole which occupies the earth.

In our own society, the idea of absolute ownership of land, as distinct from the enjoyment of certain limited rights over it, only emerged gradually with the break-up of feudalism and the development of commercial farming. This development simultaneously made the land into a straight business asset, and deprived most of the poor of any foothold on it. This in turn led to a change in perception, so that land came to be treated as a commodity.

The relationship of a human community to the land it occupies will eventually have to be rethought. In the meantime, since the land problem underlies the housing problem, government must define its role as community trustee.

The bad functioning of the present system has been most obvious in Britain as in other countries in the case of land on the fringes of towns and cities needed for development. It is here that the clash between the private commodity view of property and the public interest is most acute.

Growth of towns means a change of use from agriculture to industry and housing, and this means a rocketing of land prices, if the price is left to the market system. Colossal gains have been possible for speculators, and land is withheld in expectation of future gains.

Successive British governments have tried to tackle this problem, with policies based on doctrines either of more government action, or of less. What is needed however is not a doctrine of 'more' or 'less', but a clear doctrine of the government's role as a trustee of land. Policies should then be crystal clear, and just as tough as necessary.

We have much to learn from other European countries in this respect:

In **Holland**, there is no speculative market at all in development land, and in comparison with other countries the difference between the price of agricultural land near the city and far from the city is insignificant. All development land is acquired by the municipality at existing market prices well in advance of development. The Expropiation Act of 1851 on which this acquisition is based was designed to ensure an adequate supply of land for building, and also to safeguard the rights of landowners.

In **Sweden**, a successful public land acquisition

policy has been carried out over the past 50 years. All development land is acquired in advance, swiftly and often secretly, by an experienced Land Agent, acting for each municipality. Large land reserves are thus created which ensure an adequate supply, and the central government encourages land acquisition through loans on condition that land prices are reasonable, and a five-year reserve of land is acquired.

In **Denmark**, there is an unusual combination of tough state action and maximum individual initiative. This system is based on the preparation of regional plans for urban growth for the next 12 years. Plans are drawn up for provision of infrastructure in designated areas and local authorities are forbidden to provide infra-structures elsewhere. The land is not taken into public ownership; but landowners are charged a tax levy on their land at the time of the planning decision, as if it were already urban. At the same time, they are offered a mortgage to pay the tax if they wish to take advantage of it. Some land-owners sell to developers, others develop themselves. The payment in advance ensures rapid development to realise the increased value.

Common to all these successful systems is that the rules are simple, comprehensive and clear cut. They enable the land authority to maintain an adequate supply, and leave plenty of scope for free initiatives; there is a working partnership between government as a trustee of land and the housing market.

Public acquisition of development land is only a means to the end of responsible trusteeship. If this trusteeship is not defined, public ownership of land is of no value. If local authorities acquire land and trade in it for profit they are no different from any other developer. Their task so far as housing is concerned is to release land at a fair price to individual users or to housing associations, co-operatives or builders, in order that the supply of houses should increase, and the right to a home should be maintained.

We have considered two contrasting responsibilities of
government in relation to housing: the need on the
one hand to localise control and responsibility and
oil the market, and on the other to exercise strict
control in the name of the community over the supply
of land. In between these two there is a third function, closely allied to the other two, but more subtle
and more challenging; and that is the task of enabling.

Government in fact (if not by right) holds enormous power and responsibility for planning, construction, and major services. It is confronted by a population which has to a large extent lost its capacity to
help itself; and the power of the government and the
powerlessness of the people are of course interdepen-
dent. It is, however, possible for government, especially at local level, to change from being a disabler
to being an enabler. The subtleties of this new role
can best be conveyed by telling a story.

The Lewisham initiative began with friendship between an architect, Walter Segal, and an Assistant
Borough Architect, Brian Richardson. Both shared
beliefs about housing which are embodied in this
chapter, and both wished to do something to realise
these beliefs. Segal had already over a period of many
years developed techniques suitable for self-build
groups; Richardson has been searching for a way out
of the trap of endless provision of standard houses for
the masses.

The Labour Council, with the strong backing of
the Chairmen of the Planning Committee and the
Housing Committee, authorised a group of self-
builders to be assembled and selected four sites — an
eccentric mixture of various kinds of conventionally
unbuildable land: a steeply sloping hillside of treach-
erous clay at Forest Hill, two pieces of scrap land left
over from a reduced re-development area in Syden-
ham, and the exotic suburban garden of a villa on the
Bromley border.

100

The Public Relations Officer of the council published an advertisement in its newspaper *Outlook* inviting people on the council's waiting list or transfer lists to write for more details if they were interested in a self-build scheme. A large public meeting was held in July 1976 at which Walter Segall explained his self-build system; and as a result a steering group of potential self-builders got together with the council's officers and drew up the following proposals:

1. Applicants were to be allowed to join the scheme irrespective of age or income.
2. The scheme should be open to all, irrespective of building skills.
3. No capital would be required from the self-builders.
4. Each builder would be responsible for his own home, co-operating only on communal tasks such as main drains, fencing, paths, etc.
5. There would be a guaranteed council mortgage for self-builders wishing to purchase their houses on completion.
6. The scheme should be on some form of equity sharing basis, (part individually owned, part local authority owned).

There were so many applicants that the first group of 14 self-builders were selected by lot. None, except one plumber had any building skills. They were a miscellaneous bunch of ordinary south Londoners who were alike only in their passionate desire to escape from their present housing conditions (a 22nd floor tower block flat, an eight-storey corridor-access concrete slab block and so on) into something resembling a home.

Enormous delays then ensued while the bureaucratic machine endeavoured to cope with this strange organism. The perseverance of the group was extraordinary. When finally they were allowed to start work in March 1979, Brian Richardson says "They hurled themselves into the work faster than materials could be supplied."

The basic structure of the houses is of timber frame, with an infill of standard size panels. The houses stand on 'stilts', each foot standing on a 2 foot square concrete pad. There are no footings, the site does not have to be levelled and trees nearby do not have to be felled. The actual carpentry involves little more than the ability to saw and drill straight and true, and nothing more complex than a half-housing joint need be mastered. After the pads have been made and the timber cut, the frames can be erected within two hours. The roof is then immediately covered in, so that there is a covered space for subsequent work.

For all the simplicity of the design, the work was a saga which no-one involved will forget. It was all carried out at weekends and in the evenings. The District Surveyor recorded "If I'd been on the site, I'd have given up. We went there one day to see how Bill was getting on and we couldn't see him. He was down this hole, two feet wide, digging with a little coal shovel, and getting the earth out in a bucket."

Building was a family affair, with women and children participating on site. Each family was responsible for building its own house and their decision to undertake some work communally — such as laying drains, erecting structural frames and moving and stacking deliveries of materials — was made informally. Each family knew that it would be responsible for the maintenance of its own house and knew every inch of the fabric.

Walter Segal worked out individual designs with each family on the basis of a common method. He supplied the self-builders with basic freehand plans and sections with a typewritten specification nine pages long describing the sequence of construction; and together with his assistant, Jon Broome, he con-
102

tinuously visited the sites during the construction to discuss problems and modifications.

Technically speaking, the houses were built as 'Council houses', and the self-builders contracted to build them. On completion the self-builder was granted a 99 year lease and the council has undertaken to grant a mortgage on 50% of the final valuation, less a pre-payment equivalent to the notional value of the self-builder's labour. The other 50% remains in council ownership, the self-builder paying half the 'reasonable' rent, based on current council rents for conventional housing stock, but the self-builders can buy further 10% instalments of the council's share until they have acquired the whole property.

The completed houses are immaculately kept inside and out. The style has been described as a genuine 'modern vernacular', possessing a harmony and diversity that arises naturally from the encounter between human creativity and readily available resources.

Like all parables, the Lewisham story contains many lessons. There is a very special reason for expressing these particular lessons in parable form. As with employment there is a complicated interface problem — the interface between the sphere of public management and control, and the sphere of self-determination and creativity. If the management and control model is seen as hostile to self-determination, and is not kept within strict bounds, it extends into the heartland of human creativity, and destroys action at its source. If the management and control system is seen as an enabling one, releasing energies and promoting self-determination, then the benefits can be immense; but the interface problems will always remain, and can only be resolved piecemeal through experience, through transactions at the interface.

From these transactions we can however distil a general wisdom and begin to clarify the right roles of the various participants in the housing process.

Central government has a role to play in devising

the rules of the game, and enacting planning and building regulations. But these regulations, like the rules of all good games, should define the boundaries of freedom rather than seek to control what is done within these boundaries.

Local authorities have a role to play both as planner and as communal purchasers in providing large-scale services such as roads and sewerage; but these services should be provided in a way that leaves maximum scope for variation in the way people use them.

Large-scale industry has a role to play. Our children have been skilfully provided by industry with simple sets of foolproof construction components like Tinkertoys and Lego. Why have adults not received the same service? With the development of light, cheap and strong materials, there is now a real possibility of standardised and flexible construction set kits which will give parents the same chances as their children.

Finally, people have a role to play by fulfilling their needs and ability to create and occupy their own appropriate living space on the surface of the earth.

Chapter Seven
ENERGY: THE PROBLEMS

The duty of government to maintain and promote human rights must have a long-term dimension; it cannot ignore the rights of children, or of future generations. In this respect, it must therefore act as a *trustee of resources* for the future of mankind.

It is particularly in relation to the energy problem that this perspective has become clear to the present generation, and for this reason in the next two chapters we shall look more closely at the implications of a trusteeship approach to energy policy.

ENERGY AND INDUSTRIAL SOCIETY

Energy is fundamental to our way of life. The present shape of our industry, our transport, our agriculture, our government and social organisation, all depend on energy supply.

The sun is the motor which drives all the mechanical and life processes of our planet. The source of this energy is nuclear fusion in the sun's core. This is like an everlasting hydrogen bomb, in which matter is transformed into energy. Because of this the sun is losing mass at the rate of 6 million tonnes a second, and the temperature at its core is $12,000,000°C$. Energy radiates outwards from this inferno, becoming rapidly more diffuse and reaching us eventually mainly in the form of visible radiation that we call light. When it reaches the outer edge of the earth's atmosphere, its power is about 1.4 kilowatts per square meter. This is the total 'solar flux'. A third of this flux is reflected back into space, and more is absorbed as it passes through the earth's atmosphere. Of the energy which actually reaches the earth's surface, two thirds again is radiated back in the form of light or heat.

It is on the remaining fraction — the energy not reflected back — that which the whole of the earth's life processes depend. It is this energy which evaporates water and causes rain to fall, and which drives the winds, the waves and ocean currents; it this energy which fuels the process of photosynthesis, the beginning of life forms. All of this can be regarded as our *energy income* — it has arrived regularly for millions of years and will do so for millions more.

One tenth of the amount of energy used by wind, rain and ocean currents is used to build up life forms through photosynthesis. Plants on the surface of the sea and land build up 'organic' matter, mainly from carbon dioxide, water and nitrogen, using the sun's light energy as a fuel; and in the process they lock some of the sun's energy into the loose chemical bonds of organic matter. These bonds can be broken, and the energy used by the plant for its life processes, or other living things can feed on the plants and absorb their energy.

Some of this organic matter has been deposited and compressed in the earth's crust to form fossil fuels. Fossil fuels — oil and coal — contain the stored energy of the solar flux, accumulated over millions of years of geological time. These fuels are more efficient as energy sources than the unfossilised organic material from which they originated. They thus represent a unique store of *energy capital* which once consumed can never be replaced.

The outstanding characteristic of our industrial society is the exploitation of these fossil fuels.

Through our control and use of this energy capital, every man, woman and child in the world has the equivalent in energy of 20 hard working slaves — building our houses, transporting us to and fro, processing our food, keeping us warm, manufacturing our consumer foods, and so on. But of course this energy use is by no means equally distributed. About a third of the world's population have no energy slaves but themselves, and another third only benefit marginally from the energy bonanza. This means that most of the rest of us in industrialised societies have more like 50 energy slaves — and jet-set executives more like 200.

Throughout the period of industrialisation the trend has until recently been towards less and less efficient use of energy, and to replace human labour with energy-capital.

Take agriculture and food production. Traditionally, the farmer or the herdsman is the person who gathers and channels the sun's energy to meet human needs. It has been estimated that Philippino wet rice farming (paddy fields) produces 16 times as much energy in food as the human energy expended in planting and harvesting the crop. The herdsman harvests the sun's energy stored in grass by using it for cattle feed.

Modern farming works on a completely different system. The increase in agricultural productivity on which we pride ourselves depends very largely on a heavy input of energy in the form of fertilisers, pesticides and farm machinery (all dependent on fossil fuels). On top of this there are considerable inputs of energy for processing, packaging and transport before food gets into the shops. Energy calculations show that the food in our shops has cost twice the amount of energy to produce as it can yield. Battery eggs cost seven times as much energy as they yield; the British fishing fleet costs twenty times as much.

The shape of the houses we live in and the factories and offices we work in show the same dependence on energy supplies. The typical modern office block with huge windows pours out heat into the atmosphere, while their inhabitants loll in superheated comfort.

The sprawl of a modern town shows the same total dependence on high energy inputs. Former human settlements were always compact like a mediaeval city; a place for people, in which everywhere is within easy walking distance of the centre. Modern towns spread out in all directions, with miles and miles of roads, sewers, cables and the other paraphernalia of industrial society — all on the assumption that energy will always be available on tap to meet our needs.

The transportation explosion of the past century has transformed our conception of space and time; few people feel a bond to their own locality; and most of us are accustomed to thinking that the whole country is readily accessible to us, and other countries are for special holiday excursions.

The whole of our industrial society is like a great stew-pot seething away over a fossil fuel fire — demanding continuous supplies of concentrated energy to keep it bubbling. It requires huge imputs of energy for the tidal flow of people in and out and round about, for the industrial plant on which it depends, and for the 'services' needed to keep human beings alive within it.

HISTORICAL PERSPECTIVE

The rise of human civilisation is often described in terms of the development of tools. It seems clear that man distinguished himself from subhuman primates by the use of spears and knives, and our civilisation depends on the machinery invented in the industrial revolution.

It would however be just as appropriate to see human civilisation in terms of the *channelling of*

108

energy. Subhuman animals in general only have the energy of their own bodies to work with. Human beings through the use of tools discovered how to refine and concentrate their own physical energy, just as the point of a spear concentrates the energy of the arm.

Subsequently, through the use of fire, man was able to control and use some of the chemical energy stored in plants; then, through the invention of the waterwheel and the windmill, he began to channel some of the vast flux of solar energy for his own purposes.

The industrial revolution of the nineteenth century, which laid the foundations of modern industrial society, depended largely on the availability of iron; and iron could only be smelted on a large-scale when fossil fuels came to be used as a smelting fuel, as a result of the development of underground coal mining in the eighteenth century. By the beginning of the nineteenth century, objects that we now take as commonplace like nails, screws and chains became widely available, and there followed the development of mechanical engines and the growth of factories, built out of coal-smelted iron and fuelled by coal furnaces. Industrial towns sprang up on the coal-fields, and we became an industrialised society. Whereas in the early middle ages 90% of the population worked on the land, by 1800 50% of these had moved into the towns, and by 1900 only 10% worked on the land. This shift was due entirely to the growth of industry, which depended on coal.

Coal is a highly concentrated energy source. Every coal miner in 1900, with an average productivity of 200 tonnes per annum, mined in a year as much energy as is produced by 150 acres of forest.

There was however another fossil fuel to follow which was even more concentrated, and even more convenient; and that was oil. It was easier to mine, had a 50% higher calorific value, was more flexible in

109

its use, more easily transportable. A wave of oil industrialisation followed the wave of coal industrialisation.
World oil production had just begun at the beginning
of this century with a mere 20 million tonnes annual
output, but this amount doubled every ten years.

The oil age was also the transportation age. Coal
gave us steam engines and the railways, but oil power
gave us the internal combustion engine and the amaz-
ing growth of motor transport which we now take for
granted.

On the basis of fossil fuel energy, *electricity* was
developed commercially at the end of the nineteenth
century and rapidly became the most magical and
flexible of all energy forms, reaching into every home
and factory in the land, where it sets in motion lights,
washing machines, vacuum cleaners, television sets,
and a host of other gadgets at the flick of a switch.

What we tend to forget, however, is that the source
of nearly all this energy is fossil fuel. As the lights
burn, the television entertains us and the electric fire
warms our toes, coal and oil are burning in a power
station far away to make this possible — generating
perhaps ten times as much energy as we are using due
to inefficiencies of the plant, losses in transit, and
inefficient use by ourselves.

In the 1960s it looked as if yet a further leap forward in scientific technology would enable us to generate electricity without depending on fossil fuels.
The development of the atom bomb for destructive
purposes during the second world war was man's first
venture into a completely new form of energy production.

Among the substances of which every planet is
composed there are some which are 'radioactive'.
Radioactive substances are sources of energy, and the
energy which they emit is due to the disintegration
of atoms.

That is the basic principle of nuclear power plants,
which began to supply some of our electricity in

1956, when the first commercial nuclear power station in the world was opened at Calder Hall in Cumberland. This was a 'Magnox' reactor, and was the first of eight to be built under the First British Nuclear Programme. It has now been operating for 25 years.

In 1964, the Second British Nuclear Programme was announced, based on a new kind of reactor (The Advanced Gas Cooled Reactor). This programme has been beset by a series of technical and financial difficulties, and no AGRs have yet been commissioned. In 1979 however, Mr. David Howell, the Secretary of State for Energy, announced a proposal to construct sufficient nuclear plants to generate 15 G.W. — about 20% of the estimated energy requirement by the end of the century.

PROBLEMS: INCREASING COSTS

It has been common until recently to assume that economic growth is the principle objective of industrial society, and since this growth up to now has been entirely based on energy consumption, it has naturally been assumed that more growth means consuming more and more energy. Where will this energy come from?

The commonly accepted strategy has been a rapid expansion in the production of coal, oil and gas; a substantial development of the nuclear programme and long-term research on fusion power as the ultimate 'clean' energy source.

If government is to act as a trustee of the world's resources, it must take a long-term view. Its responsibility is not only to present generations, but also to future generations. Time horizons have been oddly affected by living with modern science. On the one hand, we talk about galaxies thousands of light years distant, of the origins of the world billions of years in the past, and its projected heat death billions of years in the future. Yet at the same time, we do not consider what will be happening to our great grandchildren

111

on this planet in a hundred years time. The responsibility of government as trustee is to take such a view.

The basic problem when we take a long-term view is that the fossil fuel which we are now using to keep the pot boiling is limited in quantity, and is rapidly being consumed. There are differences between the different types of fossil fuel. Coal will probably last at least for the twenty first century, whereas oil will by the middle of the twenty-first century be a rare and precious substance, no more to be used for burning up to keep warm than you would use diamonds for Christmas decorations. But in either case, in the longer time scale in which we expect a good trustee to function, we are depleting the basic capital resources of the earth thousands of times more rapidly than ever before in the history of the world.*

If the citizens of the twenty-second century were properly represented, how would we account to them for assuming the right to consume these resources? One answer would be to say that we foresaw a series of replacement fuels, and that we worked hard at developing them. We need to look carefully at the evidence that would support this position.

If we consider the historical series of primary energy sources that have been exploited by industrial society, we can see that they fall into a pattern. First came coal mined close to factories; then Middle East oil; then oil under the sea, then nuclear power. In each case there is a move to less and less *accessible* fuels, involving higher capital costs and more centralised production. The investment required in relation to the quantity of energy delivered is *200 times* as great for nuclear electricity as for Middle East oil.

On a world wide scale we are in the same position as many simpler societies which depend on burning wood. To begin with, they collect the wood nearby;

---

* The same argument applies, in different degrees, to all non-renewable resources, such as iron, copper, or uranium. All metals are 'precious'.

but as time goes on supplies diminish, trees are felled, and longer and longer journeys have to be made for the collection of fuel, until the journeys become a kind of slavery.

Although are situation is more complex, we have the basic problem of requiring more and more energy to tap less and less accessible energy sources. Inevitably, this shows up in ever-rising capital costs, and ever-increasing inflation. If we follow this line of development, we eventually reach a situation where a large proportion of the energy produced is needed to get more energy.

But energy is not an end, it is a means to an end; you can't eat it or drink it or in any way enjoy it 'neat'. If you spend most of your energy getting energy, you will certainly starve, and runaway inflation would be the warning signal that this situation was approaching.

There are some signs that we are already in the early stages of this situation. A leading U.S. energy expert, Dr. Barry Commoner, showed recently that for every dollar invested in energy production in 1960, 2,250,000 BTUs of energy were produced. In 1970, says Commoner, every dollar invested was only producing 2,168,000 BTUs of energy. Just three years later, in 1973, the figure had dropped to 1,845,000 BTUs for each dollar invested. In just thirteen years there had been a decrease of 18 per cent in the productivity of capital in energy production (The data adjusted for inflation). A further study of the course of inflation undertaken by the Exploratory Project for Economic Alternatives showed that in the basic consumer necessities for transport, heating, food, housing and health care — rising prices were tied to the increased costs associated with energy resources.

It was once hoped that nuclear energy would get us out of this vicious circle by providing cheap electricity, by releasing the enormous pent up energy of the atom; and now similar claims are being made for
113

nuclear fusion. In theory, there could be a technical breakthrough that would release a large amount of energy from a new source with an economical input. But the history of nuclear fusion, and the likely development of nuclear fusion, suggests that the pattern of ever-increasing costs will continue.

In the 1950s, because of the high hopes of nuclear power, 100 times more public money was spent in research and development in this field than in any other field of energy research. Yet the programme has suffered from a long series of set-backs, and cost estimates have continuously increased. Official estimates of the possible contribution of nuclear power to the energy needs have fallen by 70% in the past 10 years, and the C.E.G.B. have found themselves increasingly on the defensive about capital costs. Sir Kelvin Spencer, former Chief Scientist of the Ministry of Power, described the confidence of scientists and technicians that all the snags and hazards would yield to research and development as 'inexcusable arrogance'.*

In 1981 a Select Committee on Energy questioned the historic cost accounting basis on which nuclear investment was justified, and warned of the appalling consequences to the taxpayer and electricity consumer if further delays and breakdowns occurred as on the Isle of Grain.

Nuclear fusion, the next big technology fix in line, involves fusing hydrogen nuclei in a process similar to that which powers the sun. The theory again is good, as hydrogen exists in virtually unlimited quantities in the oceans. Yet already engineering problems can be foreseen which dwarf anything envisaged for nuclear fusion. Even the optimists and enthusiasts for fusion power now agree that 2025 is the earliest possible target date for any commercial fusion power. The hydrogen-boron reactor, which could be fuelled with 'limitless' sea water, has a reaction temperature of 3 billion degrees centigrade. The containment of

* Resurgence, May-June 1980, p. 9.

114

such temperatures involves engineering problems far beyond any existing technology, and the disposal of waste heat alone presents a problem of gigantic proportions.

It seems therefore as if there is still an underlying trend, as we would expect, towards increasing cost and decreasing returns.

PROBLEMS: INCREASING DEVASTATION

The problem however is even greater than this approach suggests. It is not only the case that more energy has to be put in to the process to get less out; it is also the case that as large-scale energy technology develops the area of associated damage increases. By analogy with the second law of thermodynamics, order can only be created at the cost of disorder elsewhere.*

If we light a fire under a cooking pot in a field, we produce a little disorder. Wood burns to ash, and half a century of growth dependent on sunlight goes up in smoke. We create an area of scorched grass, we kill some insects, and we produce a little smoke which may give us sore eyes; but we have a good meal, and the grass soon grows again. With coal mining, it is rather different. Large areas of country are covered with waste, many buildings are destroyed, and men are often killed — not necessarily counted in the capital cost.

What of nuclear power?

A nuclear power station — superficially — appears clean and safe when compared with a coal mine. Its life however is only about 25 years. After this it leaves a rather long and dangerous patch of scorched grass, because it is highly radioactive and impossible to dismantle or neutralise. It must be sealed, abandoned, and guarded against human entry for several hundred years.

* For an impressive elaboration of this thesis see *Entropy*, Jeremy Rifkin, Viking Press, New York, 1981.

The fuel of nuclear power plants is uranium, and in the course of extraction uranium miners are exposed to radioactive gases, which are likely to cause many deaths in the long-term as well as genetic damage. The same risk to a lesser degree applies to all those exposed to radiation leakage from a nuclear plant, which however could be massive in the case of accident.

Perhaps the most serious and most long-lasting associated disorder of all is the problem of waste disposal. Radioactive waste materials have to be safely 'contained' until they can be safely released. For the most common products of fission — strontium 90 and caesium — the period of containment should be about 600 years (twenty 'half-lives').

During this period they generate heat and are highly corrosive. They must therefore be stored in safe and refrigerated corrosion-proof tanks. Burial deep underground raises problems of possible contamination of the water supply and burial in casks at sea could result in spreading radioactivity through oceans. Even firing the wastes out into space by rockets has been proposed, but would be the most expensive, energy-intensive and dangerous waste disposal system ever imagined by man.

It appears that we are on an energy treadmill that is dangerous and wasteful, and which will leave a depleted and contaminated world to our descendants. This raises the problem of trusteeship in an acute form for the present generation.

Chapter Eight
ENERGY: BUILDING THE BRIDGE

It is short-sighted to burn up in the way we have been doing the energy capital of the planet, even if we think it could go on for 50 to 100 years; and it is the government's job as a trustee of resources to ensure that we do not do so. Our long-term objective must be to change the energy base of society from energy capital to energy income, as defined in the opening section. We must learn to support our way of life by using renewable energy resources, and if possible returning some of the reserves to the earth which has been pillaged for short-term needs.

This being the long-term objective, the immediate objective must be to construct a bridge which will lead from where we are now to where we need to get to; i.e. in energy terms from a capital spending to an income spending society.

There are two essential preliminaries to the building of this bridge. The first is energy conservation to stabilise the ground on this side, and to buy time. The second is the exploration of what lies on the other side.

CONSERVATION

Included in conservation policy are all measures to

reduce waste — that is energy use which is unnecessary to the objective sought.

A direct consequence of the short-sightedness of previous policies is that the wastage of energy in the present system is colossal, and therefore the potential for conservation is equally colossal. All research carried out in recent years has confirmed this view. Reducing waste is not the same as reducing output or lowering living standards. The United Kingdom (in 1965) used twice as much energy per unit of output as Japan, W. Germany and Sweden — and more than four times as much as Switzerland.*

In 1979, the Shell Petroleum Company issued a report on Energy Efficiency. The report considered what would be the impact of introducing energy efficiency systems which were sensible on purely *economic* grounds — i.e. which were likely to bring a return on investment within an 'economic lifetime' of 15-25 years. The conclusion was that in 1975, in the whole of Western Europe 30% of energy could have been saved by these means without any change in standards of living.

It is worth looking at two areas of energy consumption — domestic and transport — to illustrate the point.

Domestic

Housing is the largest consumer of energy, after industry. It accounts for 30% of primary energy use, 40% of electricity consumption, and most of the peak electricity load and requirements for power station capacity.

85% of the final energy consumption in the home is used for space and water heating, and the greatest economies in the home can be made by insulation. During the energy 'bonanza', when costs were not counted, houses were built with little regard for energy conservation. Large expanses of single glazed windows

* *Jobs for Tomorrow*, Stahel & Reday, Vantage Press 1981.

and uninsulated roof spaces are good devices for warming up the neighbourhood, but not the occupants of a house. Heating uninsulated houses or other buildings is like leaving the hot tap on in a bath instead of putting the plug in.

It has been calculated that, with an investment of money that would be recovered in real cash terms within 10 years, 35% of the heat loss through the building fabric of all existing U.K. housing could be prevented.*

As regards new buildings, there are many opportunities for energy conservation in design and construction which add very little to the costs — such as careful attention to the shape of the windows, the orientation, the interior layout and even tree planting, which contribute to energy conservation and seldom cost anything at all. By such measures, and improved insulation, houses built in 1990 and thereafter could without substantial additional cost achieve a 50% reduction in heat loss as against 1976 levels.

Comparison between countries with different insulation standards reveals staggering differences. A survey of houses in the Netherlands for instance, showed an average use of 12 kilowatts to maintain a room temperature of 21°C in an external temperature of −10°: whereas in Sweden, a similar survey of specially designed apartments in the Ostberga district of Stockholm, showed a need for only 2.2 kilowatts to maintain a normal room temperature in an external temperature of −18°. These apartments could be kept warm in a Swedish midwinter with little more than the immediate heat from lights, cooking, and the pilot lights from gas appliances.

Transport

Transport — the movement of people and goods around the surface of the earth (and recently off its

---

* *A Low Energy Strategy for the United Kingdom*, Gerald Leach, International Institute for Environment & Development, 1979.

surface!) — is the most obvious 'symptom' of industrialised society. It is by far the most rapidly rising consumer of energy. Between 1953 and 1976 passenger movement per capita in Britain doubled (from 4,200 to 8,300 km/year) but movement by car leaped six-fold, with the car population increasing from 2.8 million to just over 14 million in roughly two decades. From a four-mode system of bus, car, rail and bicycle (in that order) Britain has moved to a 'one and two halves' system of car, bus and rail, with the two halves in gradual and heavily subsidised decline.* Private transport accounts for most of this growth; freight transport has grown more slowly. Of the total increase in energy consumption since 1958, half can be accounted for by increase in transport.

As with housing, the possibilities of saving in this field are enormous, for the same historical reasons. As long as there was no perceived energy problem, cars, like houses, were designed with little regard for economy. Of the total energy released in the cylinder of a standard car, only 6% is delivered to the tyres in the form of useful work. The rest of the energy is dissipated on the way as indicated in the upper part of the diagram opposite. At every part in this chain, substantial economies are possible. Again it is a question of checking the plug rather than running hot water continuously into the bath. Some of the more dramatic economies which are possible include Constantly Variable Transmission (CVT) which would ensure that the engine is always running at its most efficient speed, and development of the Stirling 'open combustion' engine which offers very high efficiency with low pollution and noise.

The economies realistically attainable by the year 2025 are indicated in the lower half of the chart. These figures were agreed in consultation with leading engineers in the motor vehicle industry.

* Gerald Leach, op cit, p. 134.

Energy flow in a 'typical' car

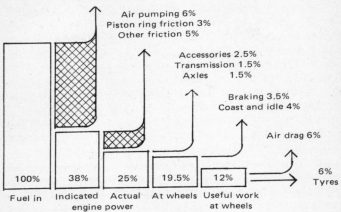

Exhaust 33%
Cylinder cooling 29%

Air pumping 6%
Piston ring friction 3%
Other friction 5%

Accessories 2.5%
Transmission 1.5%
Axles 1.5%

Braking 3.5%
Coast and idle 4%

Air drag 6%

6% Tyres

100%	38%	25%	19.5%	12%
Fuel in	Indicated engine power	Actual engine power	At wheels	Useful work at wheels

Potential fuel savings for cars

1	Air drag	5-6%
2	Tyre drag and inflation	2-2.5%
3	Idle-off and coasting	4-5%
4	10% shift in average weight	9%
5	Engine lubricants	3%
6	Transmission lubricants	3%
7	Petrol changes	5-10%
8	Electronic controls	3-7%
	Sub-total	30-38%
9	Engine design	20%
	Sub-total	44-50%
10	Continuously variable transmission (excluding 3 and 6)	10-20%
	Total	46-57%

Charts reprinted from Gerald Leach, op cit., by kind permission of the author.

The possible impact of conservation in the use of resources was calculated by the International Institute for Environment and Development in 1979.*

Electricity, being the most wasteful form of energy, has the greatest amount of slack and therefore the greatest potential for economy. After many years of rapid growth, at about 7% per year, consumption slowed to 4-5% per year in 1973 and has been roughly static ever since. Looking forward 40 years an energy conservation policy would mean a more or less static demand for electricity, with growth in some sectors such as rail electrification being cancelled out by decline in others, such as domestic heating. Even without a firm conservation policy, the price mechanism (if it were allowed to operate) would ensure that demand remained depressed. We are already in the early stages of this process, as people opt out of electrical heating and the CEGB continuously revises its demand estimates in a downward direction.

The consequence of this projection for power station construction is that the short term danger is over-capacity due to failure of the industry to appreciate and adjust to long-term trends. In January 1978 over-capacity (i.e. a generating capacity above peak load in 1977) was already 35%, and construction programmes at present envisaged will increase this. Over-capacity (if paid for by the consumer) results in even higher prices, less demand and more overcapacity, and could lead to economic failure and a failure of the electricity supply system to provide even the energy which it is in fact best suited to provide. The case for the nuclear power programme is weak on these grounds.

Oil consumption also will fall substantially both in the medium and in the long term, due partly to the phasing out of oil heating in domestic and commercial buildings by 2000 or electricity generation by 2025;

* Gerald Leach, op. cit, p.

demand for oil for transport on the other hand will continue to rise and peak in 1990, falling to present consumption levels in the early years of the next century, by which time we shall be using every year about 10% of estimated reserves.

Coal consumption will rise, but at a much more modest rate than is at present estimated by the National Coal Board's 'Plan for Coal'. It will be used increasingly in industry as a replacement for oil and gas, but this will be to some extent offset by a decline in domestic use and in electricity production. Coal reserves are substantial when compared to oil. U.K. reserves could continue to supply the projected requirement until the latter part of the twenty-first century, though of course not without substantial costs in terms of damage to buildings and sewers, and pollution and transport problems.

Because of these reserves, coal has a very important role to play in the bridge-building energy strategy. It *can* 'last' until the new income system is established. Moreover, coal technology is now experiencing a revolution which is vastly increasing energy efficiency, and flexibility of use. Coal can be a source both of liquid and of gaseous fuel. A most important development is the 'fluidised bed' system of burning coal*, which has a very high efficiency. Fluidised bed combusters are already available in Sweden, together with district heating networks and heat pumps, would heat as many houses as a billion dollar coal gasification plant, but would use only two-fifths as much coal, cost half to two-thirds as much to build and burn more cleanly than a normal power station.

Fluidised bed combustion moreover can work both on a large scale for industry or as a small household device, and can be adapted to other fuels than coal.

---

* Fluidised beds are simple, versatile devices that add the fuel a little at a time to a much larger mass of small, inert, red hot particles — sand on ceramic pellets — kept suspended as an agitated fluid by a stream of air continuously blown up through it from below.

The comparative inefficiency with which we have been burning coal and other fuels up to now is just another example of the 'slack' that can now be taken up so that we can buy time to move into an energy income society. Since coal is a principal plank in the 'bridge', government policy as a trustee of resources must be to ensure the best use of coal for the next 100 years. This policy should include appropriate oiling of the market system. The construction of new power stations based on nuclear fuel contradicts this policy, since it could diminish the market for coal, and cause premature closures of mines.

Conservation can consolidate the ground on which we stand. What of the land on the other side?

THE OTHER SIDE: ENERGY INCOME

The earth's energy income, as distinct from its capital, is either in the form of direct solar radiation, or derived from this radiation. Of the total solar radiation arriving at the outer boundaries of the earth's atmosphere, about 65% re-appears in the form of

- terrestial heat
- Evaporation and precipitation (including the flow of rivers and waterfalls)

124

— wind, wave, convection and ocean currents, and
— photosynthesis, the process by which plants grow.

Additional to these virtually inexhaustible energy sources originating from the sun is geothermal energy, which comes from the earth's interior and ultimately radiates into outer space.

These are the income energy sources which lie on the 'other side'. Research in energy technology in all these fields is advancing rapidly, and it is impossible to give more than the briefest indication here of long-term possibilities.

Wind power, until recently neglected by government and dismissed as somewhat freakish, has now come closer to the centre of the stage. Plans for building the first full-scale three-megawatt wind power generator in the Orkneys was announed on January 27 by Mr. David Howell, Secretary of State for Energy. In addition, work will begin shortly on a much smaller generator of 250 kilowatts on the same site to be in operation by the end of this year.

The argument for the three-megawatt machine derives simply from the fact that the electricity board loses £8m a year supplying power to the islands, because it has to use expensive diesel generators. But the smaller machine, which will provide the experience necessary for building and operating the larger one, may soon find a market throughout the highlands and islands and on the north-east coast, Wales and south-west of Britain where the wind patterns are favourable for aero-generators.

The Central Electricity Generating Board has also announced plans for developing a 200-kilowatt machine on a lowland site at Dyfed, in Wales. The board is also investigating three sites as possible places for clusters of up to 10 large generators to be built by 1985. These may be the predecessors to huge windmill farms in shallow waters off-shore.

Direct use of sunlight for space and water heating also has a very important future, even in a country like Britain where more sunlight falls on a typical building than is required to heat it (or cool it) throughout the year (In Israel and southern parts of the U.S. it is of course already taken much for granted.) Technologies range from simply using windows as sun traps and walls as thermal stores, to solar panels with storage systems and photo-voltaic cells.

'Storage' of energy for use when needed is a crucial problem, but there could be a significant technical breakthrough ahead in this field. One approach is to store heat in salts, paraffin wax or other materials that change reversibly from liquid to solid state, so that energy can be shared and released as latent heat (as in a heat pump). Another approach is to use the heat absorbed and released in chemical reactions, as in a water/sulphuric acid system at present being investigated at the Rutherford Laboratories. A third approach has been tried in Sweden, where 50 small houses or flats are joined to a group heat store of $10,000^3$ m. in volume.

Conversion of sunlight into electricity through photo-voltaic cells is a third promising line of investigation. These cells have been used for space for 10 years. The potential advantages of this technology are considerable. There are no moving parts, a lifetime of over 100 years, little maintenance, and systems can be large or small. Present costs are 50 times more than conventional power generation, but this factor may be reduced rapidly when research and development advance and conventional generation becomes more costly.

Other forms of income energy worth serious attention include hydrogen production from water by solar chemical means, wave energy, 'biomass' (organic fuel production — like growing wood), methanol from crops, and geothermal energy. For the U.K. in particular a very important development under consideration at this time is the Severn Barrage, which will harness tidal power by creating the largest lake in Britain.

A wide range of possibilities is open therefore to provide the base for an energy income society in the latter half of the next century.*

GOVERNMENT AS RULE-MAKER AND ENABLER: STANDARD SETTING

Given the enormous scope for conservation by 'putting the plug in', it is the first responsibility of government as a trustee of resources to ensure that this is done.

The most effective form of government action in this field is that of rule-maker and enabler. Without becoming involved in purchasing or management either of the car industry or the housing industry, government can modify the rules of the game by setting performance standards for houses and vehicles.

Until 1965 there were no national building codes that restricted heat losses from dwellings. In 1965, Building Regulations established 'U-values' (maximum heat loss standards), of 1.7 for walls and 1.4 for lofts, and further reductions in permitted heat loss are now planned. The standards could gradually be increased until by 1990 the heat loss in new dwellings would be half the present permitted level.

It is also possible to introduce efficiency standards in space and water heating systems. An official approval scheme stipulating 70% full load efficiency for oil burning appliances has been operated since 1975 by the Domestic Oil Burning Equipment Testing Association (DOBETA); and the E.E.C. currently recommends a full load efficiency for all domestic boilers of 75%.

* According to a recent estimate 18% of U.K. needs could realistically be met from renewable resources by the year 2000, and 68% by 2025. Publication by D. Olivier, Earth Resources Research Ltd., 1979.

Energy performance standards for cars have not yet been introduced, and they present more difficulties, one being international competition. But the difficulties can be overcome, and the British Government is less rigorous in standard setting than most of its competitors.

Standard setting* is an important governmental rule making function. Provided it is clear and for a good purpose it is usually welcomed by industry, which can then get on with its own job, and can compete fairly in the knowledge that everyone has to stick to the same ground rules.

But what of the market?

GOVERNMENT AS RULE MAKER AND ENABLER: OILING THE MARKET

We have seen that the underlying problem in energy is the shortage of fossil fuels, and the ever-increasing difficulty and cost of tapping more remote sources in order to keep the pot boiling.

In such a case, the market mechanism of classical economics could be seen as the natural adjusting mechanism which is required. If goods are scarce and difficult to get, the price will go up, and less will be used!

To some extent this is happening. Demand for energy-efficient cars took General Motors by surprise in the USA, saddling it with massive stocks of unsaleable vehicles; and market pressures have also generated a huge amount of research and development in energy economy in the motor vehicle industry, on which most of the figures in the previous section are based. In the housing field, energy conservation is a rapidly growing sector of private business, including insulation systems, solid fuel stoves and heat pumps.

---

* It is important however to distinguish *performance* standards from *specification* standards. Performance standards lay down that a certain objective has to be achieved; specification standards say *how* it is to be achieved and can be vexatious and absurd.

However, there are important respects in which the market mechanism does not work. The Shell analysis showed what large savings could be made in energy consumption if people made sensible economic decisions about investing in conservation; but sensible economic decisions mean thinking in the fairly long-term — say 15 years. Most house owners do not think or plan on these terms. Low income groups and first time buyers are often fully stretched, and could not raise even more capital for energy conservation measures to reduce operating costs, and people in higher income groups may not count operating costs too closely, if they are only a small part of their total budget.

The price mechanism does not work well with cars either. Petrol forms only 30-40% of average motoring costs and the large amount of expense account motoring cushions the effect of rising prices. Moreover, the rise in prices has not yet in any way reflected the underlying problem, nor is it likely to do so for the next 5-10 years. A gallon of petrol in the U.K. in 1953 cost a manual worker 74 minutes of labour, in 1973 it cost 25 minutes, and in 1977 28 minutes. Economy measures, now likely to progress rapidly, will decrease demand and depress prices even further, unless OPEC drastically reduces the supply.

If the pricing system is not functioning well enough to encourage conservation, then it is appropriate for government to seek ways of oiling the mechanism. It can do this by increasing the costs of energy wastage, or increasing the benefits of energy saving.

Taxes on energy-economical devices can be reduced, and taxes on energy-wasteful devices increased; research and development into energy economy can be promoted by public money. Long term loans for energy economy in housing can be made available, as through building societies.* Direct subsidies and

* For more detailed recommendations see *In Favour of an Energy-Efficient Society*, Office for Official Publications of the European Community, 1980.

grants, as for example for insulating houses, are another option.

There is however an underlying difficulty about the relation of government and market, due to a confusion of government roles.

If industrial society were to approach a really serious emergency due to failing energy supplies, it could be argued that market forces, left to themselves, would 'solve the problem' by showing warning signals. If the cost of oil, electricity and oil-based products started doubling every year, then there would be radical changes in our whole way of life. The pot would soon stop boiling. Unfortunately, there would also be catastrophic disorder, with the collapse of all the major institutions of society which are most dependent on high energy inputs. Farmers would be unable to produce enough food, firms with heavy transport costs would become bankrupt, and most institutions with large 'catchment areas', like big shopping centres, would become derelict. Unemployment would reach nightmare proportions and social chaos would ensue. All this could be achieved rapidly by the price mechanism.

What could the government do in such a situation?

The fact is that the government is centrally involved both as purchaser and as provider in the energy business. Because of the escalating scale of energy investment, and the risks involved, it has fallen to government to carry out public purchasing functions. Only government, for instance, has the combination of funds and lack of accountability required to invest in nuclear power.

Because of this heavy government involvement, the signalling mechanism is already seriously out of order, since prices are not based on the long-run cost of new energy supply. The capital cost of new supply, as we have seen, is escalating rapidly with a large margin of uncertainty. If the electricity industry were run on conventional economic lines, the cost of building

130

nuclear power plant would have to be built into the present electricity price structure.

If a real emergency threatened, the pressures on government not to let the price signals work would be overwhelming. Direct government involvement in the purchasing and provision of energy would mean that it was directly responsible for pricing policy, and therefore apparently, for the emergency. Moreover, the government's duty to maintain order would be a powerful and legitimate argument for not letting the price signalling mechanism work, since this would lead to social breakdown. The signalling system would therefore almost certainly be jammed; disaster would strike with even less warning and the ensuing damage would be worse.

Although we are not yet anywhere near to such a catastrophe, the confusion of roles in government is already a matter of serious concern, and has prevented the proper functioning of trusteeship. A recent Study issued by the EEC* pointed out that most government intervention and regulation of the energy price mechanism has in fact been harmful to the cause of conservation. Conflicts about depletion policy in relation to British north sea oil reflect the same confusion.

It is for this reason that it is essential to distinguish the trusteeship objectives which are the prime responsibility of government, and to disentangle them from managerial objectives with which these could conflict.

TRUSTEESHIP, DECENTRALISATION AND APPROPRIATE TECHNOLOGY

What does the land look like on the other side of the bridge? What would be the shape of an energy income society? Government as trustee must ask these questions in order to plan a suitable strategy for the future.

* *In Favour of an Energy-Efficient Society*, Office for Official Publications of the European Community, 1980.

131

There are two kinds of energy income technology at present under investigation — the large-scale and the small-scale. At one extreme, an array of solar collectors occupying many square miles is planned to feed into a national grid, and to be piped to homes and offices throughout the country to keep people warm; at the other extreme, insulation, local energy storage and perhaps wearing a pullover to achieve the same objective. At one extreme, the Severn Barrage; at the other extreme, small water turbines of as little as 5 kilowatts, such as have been developed by the Intermediate Technology Development Group, which can be plugged into rivers to heat homes or power small workshops nearby. At one extreme, nuclear fusion — (which could be called an unlimited energy course); at the other extreme, stoves to burn waste materials effectively.

Neither the big nor the small technology can be ruled out in principle; but there is a built-in bias towards the big which must be corrected, and can only be corrected by a government with a long-term view.

The bias comes from history. It is partly that we are not used to counting the wastage and the disorder associated with big systems. Construction of large central systems involves distribution costs, environmental costs, social costs, and risks of catastrophic breakdown which smaller systems avoid. Even if we count the costs however there is another reason for the bias which is more difficult to correct. Industrial society, as we saw in the previous chapter, is based on large centralised energy supply systems. The shape of our cities, the size of our factories, the transportation system all depend on such centralised systems.

Looking forward to the energy income society on the other side of the divide, we can already see that it should on the whole consist of living and working units which are smaller in scale. It is improbable that anything like the modern industrial city will ever be
132

powered from energy income. Large industrial units will certainly continue to exist where large is necessary, as perhaps in the car industry. But the energy of the sun and the winds is widely dispersed, and it is costly and wasteful to collect and redistribute it on a large scale. The smaller and more local the energy source, the more efficient its use. Correcting the existing bias in favour of big technology means moving towards smaller communities which will use local energy and local resources.

There is another way in which long-term energy trusteeship points towards smaller and more localised activities.

The main symptom of the energy wasteful society is the 'boiling of the pot' — the enormous amount of sheer movement to and fro of people and goods, sometimes even from one side of the world to the other — and sometimes off the earth altogether. Dr. Schumacher once said we consider it normal to see a lorry full of bisuits with crosses on travelling south pass a lorry full of biscuits with dots on travelling north; and it is now common to commute 200 miles daily to work!

Most of this movement is not desired as such; it creates a large area of disorder in the form of environmental damage, and death and injury of people. It is also wasteful of energy, since it is impossible to move objects around without expending and wasting energy.

It is already clear that the society on the other side should be one where there is much less sheer movement. A society with less movement is one in which more human needs are met with the local community. Low energy microtechnology in communications now offers a chance of totally transforming the shape of industrial society. The long-term strategy of government as trustee should therefore be to promote especially those technologies and those forms of social and industrial development which make such a society possible. Planning and industrial policies should aim

133

to reduce journeys to work, school or public facilities.

The boiling of the pot is neither desirable nor sustainable.

TRUSTEESHIP WORLD-WIDE: THE INTERNATIONAL DIMENSION

This chapter has been primarily concerned with the government's responsibility as a trustee in the U.K.

However, just as human rights cannot be conceived as stopping at the national boundary, so the responsibilities of trusteeship must include a world-wide perspective.

This is most obviously true in the case of energy resources. The capital resources which are now being so rapidly consumed are in fact the resources of the entire world. The oil run-out date which is often calculated is not a national but a planetary phenomenon, and therefore affects the future of the entire human race.

It has been clear now for many years that the dream of universal industrialisation could never be realised. Developing countries can never build industries based on fossil fuel to the extent that industrialised nations have done, because the fossil fuel simply does not exist in those quantities, and what does exist is being rapidly consumed. Promoting high energy and high capital industry in developing countries is like getting them to climb a staircase which ends in mid-air. Already many of them spend 40% of their GNP on energy imports, and this figure is rising inexorably, and with it the burden of unmanageable debt. Development based on renewable and local energy resources is therefore even more important in a world-wide context than in a national context.

There are ways out of the dilemma — especially by the development of hydropower, and the efficient use of biomass — 'energy farming' which could revitalise rural areas, create thousands of jobs and provide a base for decentralised development; but all this

134

requires international collaboration and investment that is both imaginative and far-sighted.*

Dr. Schumacher made the interesting suggestion that a good world-wide depletion policy would be to restrict use of fossil fuels in any year to a fixed percentage of estimated reserves — say 5% of oil. This would ensure that there would never be a 'run-out' at all. Such a policy, or any other policy of responsible trusteeship world-wide would however depend on a firm international structure which at present does not exist.

A national government cannot ignore world-wide human rights and trusteeship responsibilities; but neither can it act competently on a world-wide basis. Attempting to do so can result in great confusion, as attempts are made to balance national interests against the rights of undefined populations in distant countries. For this reason it is essential to create an appropriate structure of justice to carry responsibility for human rights and trusteeship world-wide. This can be a way out of the dilemma faced by many national governments which have become too closely involved as managers and purchasers to act as good trustees. The beginnings of this international structure are already there. The World Energy Conference set up a World Energy Commission in 1975, which has now prepared a substantial report on World Energy, to the year 2020. The EEC has also made recommendations to member states on policies designed to conserve energy advising them to separate economic growth from increasing energy consumption.

If national governments are to take seriously their world responsibilities (and there is no way of avoiding them), then they have to act as midwives for a new international order. This same responsibility is evident in the field of defence which is the subject of the next two chapters.

* This argument is developed fully by P. B. Baxendell (Chairman, Shell Transport and Trading Company) in 'Energy in the 2000s — what happens to the have-nots?', 1981.

Chapter Nine
THE INTERNATIONAL DIMENSION: DEFENCE

THE RIGHT TO SELF-DEFENCE

The purpose of government is to promote and maintain human rights; but a government's authority and responsibility is normally limited to a particular patch of land. It seems sensible to say therefore that the purpose of government is to promote and maintain human rights within a certain territory. This position has its difficulties, but it is a useful starting point.

If the government's task is to maintain human rights in a certain territory, what relationship must it have with other countries?

The right to life and self-determination is the basis of the whole human rights structure, and the fundamental duty of government is therefore to defend the lives and freedom of its subjects from any force which threatens to destroy their rights. Assuming that there are forces which threaten the lives and liberties of citizens, it is evidently a primary duty of government to oppose those forces. This is equally true whether the forces threatening life and liberty are internal or external, and there may well be a close connection between internal and external forces, as we shall see later.

It is usually accepted that defending the lives and liberties of subjects must involve the use of military force; and the duty of the government to defend its citizens in this way is formulated in international law as the individual and collective right of self-defence. It is incorporated in the United Nations Charter as a right retained by states where the international system fails. Article 51 of the U.N. Charter reads as follows:

> Nothing in the present Charter shall impair the inherent right of individual or collective self-defence if an armed attack occurs against a Member of the United Nations, until the Security Council has taken measures necessary to maintain international peace and security.

The use of force by states for any purpose other than self-defence (or as an exercise of collective security under the authority of the Security Council of the U.N.) is excluded in international law. It is contrary to international law for states to use or threaten the use of force as a means of settling disputes.

The present international defence system is seen primarily in terms of nuclear deterrence between two opposing alliances, NATO and the Warsaw Pact. Both alliances would argue that these alliances are ways of exercising a right of collective self-defence.

The theory of deterrence is essentially very simple. It is that both sides possess the capacity to inflict unacceptable damage on the other in the event of an attack, and therefore an attack will not take place. The main version of this deterrent theory in the first phase of deterrence was called MAD — 'Mutually Assured Destruction'. This meant that any nuclear attack would result in massive destruction of the attacker's cities. The present form of the deterrent theory is known as 'flexible response'; it implies that each side has a ladder of weapons matching the opponent's ladder of weapons, and that this extends the deterrent effect downwards and permits a degree of control at each level.

In the perspective of human rights, this system of defence presents some difficulties.

Failure to 'defend'

The first difficulty relates specifically to the right of collective self-defence, on which the use or threat of force must be based. The purpose of defence is to preserve the life and liberty of the population, yet we are at this time involved in a considerable risk of extermination — perhaps as great as one in three during the next ten years if present policies continue. When calculating a risk we normally multiply the severity of the risk by the probability of its occurrence. It may be reasonable to incur a big risk of a small accident, or a small risk of a big. In the case of national defence the danger is so severe that even a small risk of its occurrence should rationally mean that the highest priority should be given to eliminating it.

The reason for this risk is that the deterrent system, though rationally defensible, is unstable.

The theory of Mutually Assured Destruction was that peace could be preserved indefinitely, because an act of war on either side would be suicidal. It is very probable that the non-use of nuclear weapons during the 35 years that they have been in existence is due partly to this deterrent effect. The system is unstable however because both sides are continuously improving their weapons systems both in quantity and in quality; and unless this development happens symmetrically, there is a danger of one side gaining a critical advantage that could make it 'worth-while' (no longer 'MAD') to launch a nuclear war.

The reasons for this continuous development of armaments in quality and quantity derive partly from the nature of the deterrent system, and partly from the technological and industrial process. Where national security is at risk, there is a characteristic

138

pattern of over-reaction. There is no precise answer to the question of how much military capability is 'enough', and if this capability is the sole means of security then it is better to have more than enough rather than less. At the same time the technological and scientific system is continuously generating new and 'better' weapons, and it is not easy to see how this process could be stopped.

A consequence of this development is that the massive and 'crude' nuclear weapons of the first generation are now being supplemented or replaced by much smaller and more accurate weapons, known as 'Precision-Guided Missiles'. The Cruise Missiles and the SS20 are weapons of this kind, and are designed to land within a few meters of their targets. They have come to be known as 'theatre nuclear weapons' — implying that their use can be confined to a 'theatre' of war.

According to the ladder theory of flexible response, the deterrent effect of the big bombs is spread downwards to the little ones, because of the perceived danger of escalation. However another view is that the development of 'theatre' nuclear weapons makes their actual use more likely where they can be seen to achieve some limited objective; and once they are used, the ladder would rapidly lead upwards. It was to this danger that the late Lord Mountbatten referred when he said that we were 'hurtling towards a precipice'.

A further cause of instability in the deterrent structure is that it relies on increasingly rapid responses to threat, and therefore to sophisticated information technology which is also developing rapidly. This increases the danger of war due to technological error or misinformation, such as those which led to 'red alerts' on two occasions in the United States in 1980.

THE RIGHTS OF CITIZENS OF OTHER COUNTRIES

Two other problems of the deterrent structure concern the citizens of other countries; and it is at this point that we become involved in a basic problem of definition. The government's authority is territorial; but if the government's task is to maintain and promote *human* rights, its concern cannot end at the border; if it does, then it is evidently not concerned with human rights, but with, say, British rights, or black rights, or white rights. If on the other hand we say the task of a territorial government is to maintain and promote human rights world wide, we give it an impossible task.

I shall return to this problem. For the time being, let us accept that as a matter of human experience it is impossible to halt the concern for human rights at the border; and it is also increasingly impossible in terms of international human rights law, which proclaims that individuals in every country have rights which every government must respect.

One important strand in the development of human rights law has been the Hague and Geneva Conventions to which the UK is a signatory, specifically banning the use of indiscriminate weapons of mass destruction. The same explicit prohibition of the use of such weapons is contained in authoritative statements from all the major world religions.* This is not surprising since if the 'right to life' has any meaning at all it must include the right of innocent people not to be killed.

However, the weapons on which our defence policy now depends are indiscriminate in a sense far beyond that contemplated by the Geneva Conventions. The Hiroshima bomb, after 35 years, continues to take its toll in the form of cancer and deformity; the 'target'

* E.g. Resolution of the British Council of Churches, November 1979: "The Assembly of the BBC re-affirms the conviction which the Council expressed in 1963 that nuclear weapons 'are an offence to God and a denial of His purpose for man. Only the rapid progressive reduction of these weapons, their submission to strict international control and their eventual abolition can remove this offence. No policy which does not explicitly and urgently seek to realise these aims can be acceptable to Christian conscience.' "

of a nuclear bomb includes generations yet unborn.

The purpose of possessing these weapons of mass destruction is to prevent their use. Nevertheless the structure of deterrence as we know depends on the continuous unquestioning readiness of military and political leaders to 'press the button'. 'Pressing the button' is a euphemism for a crime which could have no defence on grounds of obedience, (on the precendent of the Nuremburg Trials) vengeance or the maintenance of the values of Western Society, since these values would be negated by action allegedly carried out to maintain them.

IDEOLOGICAL INSTABILITY

There is a third major problem in the deterrent structure which also involves the rights of other countries.

In order to understand this problem it is essential to realise that the deterrent system has both a 'hardware' aspect and an ideological aspect. Each side is promoting a belief and a certain form of social system. People may vary greatly in their judgements about the relative importance of ideology and 'naked force', or 'imperialism', on either side; but what cannot be denied is that the ideology of each side is an essential part of its armoury, because it is with the help of ideologies that morale is mobilised at home and alliances are made overseas.

On either side there is ostensibly a strong commitment to human rights. Both Russia and the United States are signatories to the U.N. Covenants* on Human Rights and to the Helsinki Final Act. Both sides proclaim the principle of self-determination, and though each side has its own special variations, there is a considerable coincidence in the rhetoric of both sides concerning this fundamental principle. This is not surprising because to deny the principle of

* The U.N. Covenants are signed by the U.S.A. and the USSR; but the U.S.A. has not yet ratified these Covenants whereas the USSR (together with 60+ other states) has done so.

self-determination is to assert a right to dominate; and it would be quite imposssible to assert such a right in the present international scene without becoming an object of universal denunciation (as for example in the U.N. Assembly resolutions condemning Soviet intervention in Afghanistan). This denunciation cannot be separated from the balance of power which is at the basis of the deterrent system. Ideological mistakes lose allies.

This leads directly to the major problem of the deterrent system, which also may provide the clue to its transformation.

In military terms the deterrent structure consists of two large alliances in confrontation. These alliances are the military expression of an ideological confrontation which divides the world into opposing camps. The camps are composed of widely diverse elements; and on the fringes there are always the non-committed, the backsliders, and countries where there is internal warfare. As long as the deterrent system is seen as the basis of defence, the dominant members of the two opposing camps will be obliged to use force to hold their side together or to extend it. This means that they are obliged to deny in practice the principles of human rights and self-determination on which their systems are based. On both sides, there is now a tradition of such interventions, or attempted interventions. On the American side, Vietnam, Cuba, the Dominican Republic, Guatemala, El Salvador; on the Russian side, Hungary, Poland, Czechoslovakia, Afghanistan.

These interventions, necessary in the context of a 'bi-polar' system, are becoming increasingly counter-productive because of the vitality of national liberation movements. The deterrent system therefore has serious ideological as well as technical instability.

Human history can be seen as a series of conquests and interactions of groups seeking to expand and establish empires in a shrinking world. One logical end point of such a process of interacting powers would be a single world empire. A number of leaders had such an end in view. Hitler did; perhaps Stalin did; perhaps the United States did. A great deal of science fiction is based on this deep-rooted fantasy. It would be surprising if a world power which had a chance did not consider a bid for world empire; it would be a logical move, and as one's own motives are always good, it would be seen as the right way to the goal of world unity and justice.

However, things did not work out like that. Because force breeds counterforce, and conquest is resisted, the world arrived at a different situation — that of two 'finalists'. The East-West confrontation can be seen in that light too, as a kind of ultimate Wimbledon.

It could be argued that this is a better situation than a single world empire, because it contains an element of balance and therefore an element of justice. But nuclear weapons are no tennis balls, so we have to think again before the game goes any further. Other problems relating to human rights are dwarfed by the danger of extermination which threaten us. In the next chapter we explore the paths that may lead out of this danger.

Chapter Ten
DEFENCE: CHANGING THE MEANING

We have seen that the deterrent system is rooted in
the right of self-defence; and yet at the same time it
contains contradictions which are making it obsolete
as a way of defending any human rights, including
the right to life itself. Clearly the system must be
transformed; but we can only transform it if we first
take seriously the positive human rights meaning
which it embodies; and since the system is not just to
do with military 'hardware', but with beliefs and attitudes which give meaning to the hardware, we can
only transform it by simultaneously working at the
hardware and at the beliefs.

DISARMAMENT AND ARMS CONTROL

Disarmament and Arms Control negotiations are the
'coal face' of the international effort to reduce the
dangers of the present system by controlling the hardware. These negotiations are highly complex, and are
taking place in many different contexts. They have
been going on now for thirty years, and virtually
nothing has been achieved in the way of disarmament;
indeed, during this period armaments have increased
many times over. However, it would be a mistake to
neglect the central importance of these negotiations.

Although no significant disarmament has yet occurred, a number of binding international agreements have been entered into, and others are in sight of conclusion. Among these are the Biological and Toxin Weapon Convention (in force 1975) — the only actual disarmament treaty — which prohibits biological and toxin weapons and provides for the destruction of existing material, the Non-Proliferation Treaty (1970) which prohibits the transfer of nuclear weapons by nuclear state and the acquisition of such weapons by non-nuclear states; the Treaty of Tlatelolco (1967) which prohibits nuclear weapons in Latin-America; the Partial Test Ban Treaty (1963) which bans nuclear weapons tests in the atmosphere, in outer space and under water, and the Sea-Bed Treaty which prohibits the placement of nuclear weapons on the sea-bed outside the 12 mile zone (1972); and the Strategic Arms Limitation Talks (SALT).

Further important measures under consideration include the banning of chemical weapons (the main point still to be resolved being the automatic right of inspection on both sides) and the bilateral talks at Vienna between the Warsaw Pact and NATO on the reduction of conventional forces in Central Europe, which have now made some progress on the basic problems of how to measure existing forces as a starting-point.

Apart from these agreements, there have been some important structural advances. Since 1978 a 40-nation permanent committee on disarmament has been established at Geneva which reports annually to the General Assembly of the United Nations, and which in 1980 was chaired by China, (long excluded from all such negotiations). Another structural advance under discussion is for the setting up of a World Disarmament Authority or International Disarmament Organisation. Such an organisation would take under its wing all the control measures required by the many partial agreements; and would

145

build on this experience to take initiatives leading towards general disarmament.

What is the ordinary citizen to make of all this, and what does it signify for security?

First of all, although the achievements are apparently trivial, it would be a mistake to underestimate either the achievements or the structure within which they have taken place. The tradition of negotiation is now well-established, and has its own 'common law'*; and it is often not the arms limitation aspect of agreements so much as the control systems associated with them that are important, since these can 'pilot' more significant control systems in the future.

It is possible to see arms control and disarmament negotiations as attempts to cross an ever-widening chasm by throwing over bits of cotton attached to stones to people on the other side. But this could be a very sensible thing to do. If a stone is caught and the cotton spans the abyss, it can be used to pull over the string, and then the rope, and finally a bridge can be constructed.

Continuous public pressure must be maintained to assist the politicians in their task of negotiation. The categorisation of iniatives into 'unilateral' and 'multilateral' is unhelpful if its purpose is to label one as 'good' and the other as 'bad'. No way forward which makes sense should be eliminated by slogans. Multilateral talks could well prepare ground for unilateral initiatives and unilateral initiatives can make more sense when placed in a multilateral context.

The work at the coal face of disarmament negotiations will however only succeed if the context within which they are taking place is changed.

The kind of changes required are discussed in the following sections.

---

* Margaret Thatcher appears to have stepped outside this common law when in 1980 she raised the possibility of resuming a chemical weapons programme, in contradiction of a 20 year tradition of British diplomacy. The tradition later emerged intact.

146

'Confidence Building Measures' is a term only recently introduced into arms control and disarmament negotiations. They include measures such as mutual agreements by opponents in the deterrrent system to inform each other about military exercises and troop movements and to exchange observers.

Confidence Building Measures are an important departure in disarmament negotiations. Their purpose is to change the *meaning* of the mutual deterrent structure, so that it becomes more clear to both sides that it is a defensive and not an aggressive system. In human rights terms, this means it comes nearer to being an assertion of the right of collective self-defence, rather than a threat of domination.

Part of the difficulty with arms control and disarmament negotiations has always been that they concentrated on objects — countable weapons in certain places. Since the weapons systems are vast and complex, it is very difficult indeed to get any agreement about 'equivalence'.

The deterrent system however is not a set of things; it is a set of meanings, — which includes intentions. The meaning depends to some extent on the things; but the things can be highly ambiguous. Weapon systems can be 'read' in quite different ways; they are a bit like those puzzle pictures of staircases which can be seen either as upside down stairs coming from the ceiling, or right-way-up stairs going up from the floor.

In particular it is very hard just from looking at weapon systems today to distinguish aggression from defence; and this is particularly difficult in the case of deterrence, because deterrence means saying to the opponent 'I can attack'. It is not like wearing a bullet-proof vest, which threatens no-one; it is a system of mutual threat.

Of course the problem is not just that the system appears to be ambiguous at present, but that it *is* ambiguous. There is no doubt at all that there is a strong defensive element on both sides; but there is a certain aggressive element as well. In any case, aggression and defence are closely related psychologically as most people can verify from their own experience.

It is however *because* of this real ambiguity that Confidence Building Measures offer hope of tipping the balance. The term 'Confidence Building Measures' came into use in the Helsinki Final Act. This Act contained a commitment on the part of the two opposing alliances to notify each other of manoeuvres involving over 25,000 ground troops, and a declaration of intention to exchange observers, to give notification of military movements and to exchange military visits. These notifications have taken place; and exchanges have been invited. There have in fact been no breaches of the agreement reached at Helsinki.

This may seem a very modest achievement, but the importance of Confidence Building Measures is greater than the modest achievements suggest. To the extent that they succeed, they move the deterrent system towards an agreed symbolism. To the extent that *both* sides actually believe that *both* systems are defensive, and that their purpose is that they should not be used, they become simply a way of each side saying that it refuses to be dominated by the other; they become a ritual, rather like the ritualised 'displays' that can be observed sometimes in both human and animal behaviour.

Once this common meaning is established and agreed, a range of new possibilities of modification and control can be opened up.

Progress in Confidence Building Measures will not be rapid and dramatic, any more than it is in arms control and disarmament. There is still the difficulty that the 'deterrence' posture means a readiness for instant attack, or even 'pre-emptive' attack — for the purpose of defence. Even with notification and explanation, it is still hard to distinguish deterrent/ defence postures from aggressive postures.

There are nevertheless ways forward in confidence building which can be charted once the direction of advance is established. For instance certain measures are advocated by Jonathan Alford of the International Institute for Strategic Studies* which are designed to place obstacles in the way of an attacking force, without seriously impeding defence. These include the placement of observers in ammunition storage facilities, who would easily detect outloading prior to war; a gradual backward movement of ammunition storage sites; or a restriction on mechanical bridging equipment on forward positions, a measure that is of particular importance in central Europe where major rivers run N—S. The detailed task of clarifying these options calls for the highest level of strategic skill. This is a task for the experts. But it is for the rest of us to define the long-term objectives, and to give the experts their instructions.

Let us speculate for a moment about the implications of this process of 'symbolic transformation'.

Imagine that we advance over the next ten years to a situation where even without any significant degree of disarmament, there is an established system of mutual information exchange about military movements, agreement about force levels (as through SALT), a clear understanding on both sides of strategic doctrine, and a high degree of confidence that both sides 'intend' defence rather than military aggression. This situation would be ahead of where we are now — but it is not so far ahead as to be totally out of sight.

This situation would imply that the deterrent situation had acquired an unambiguous meaning understood by both sides. This meaning would be based on the agreed right of collective self-defence, and ultimately therefore on the principle of self-determination. The way would then be open for

* Adelphi Papers no. 149 The Future of Arms Control: Part III Confidence Building Measures.

much more far reaching modifications of the system, provided the same *meaning* was retained.

There could for instance be a long-term policy of *clustering* of weapon systems in limited and unambiguously defensive situations. The modest withdrawal of ammunition storage sites from front line positions proposed at present could be the first step towards a more ambitious withdrawal. Clustering of weapons systems could then be linked to *mutual targeting*, agreed and notified with appropriate exchange of observers. The only function of the weapons systems in question would then be clearly to neutralise the opponents weapons system — which is precisely what is meant by an agreed system of defence/deterrence. The way would then be open to a third phase of *controlled obsolescence*.

The logical conclusion of such a programme (perhaps by the middle of the twenty first century) might well be two purely symbolic weapons systems (perhaps one in Siberia and one in Arizona!) which would in fact express in a ritual form the determination of all people of the world not to submit to conquest.

A pipe dream? Maybe; but stranger transformations have taken place even in the history of our own nation. When the Speaker enters the House of Com-

mons he is preceded by a Sergeant-at-Arms carrying a golden mace — a symbol of the Queen's authority; and the mace is by origin a spiked club, designed to keep the Queen's Peace by knocking out the brains of anyone who disturbs it!

ALTERNATIVE DEFENCE

It may well be asked at this point, what becomes of the right to individual and collective self-defence when weapons systems are dismantled? Are there any other ways of defending ourselves?

Many people argue that it is unrealistic to imagine a world in which no group will seek to dominate and overpower another. They say, with good reason, that the map of the world has been shaped by conquest; there is no reason to expect human nature to change. It is not possible to eliminate modern weapons technology, and in a world deprived of the superpower deterrent structure, any aspiring tyrant could rapidly build up sufficient arms to take over the territory of an undefended neighbour, and so begin again the whole history of international conflict. For this reason, many people can only envisage world order based on a massive accumulation of military forces — whether in a single world government, or in a superpower alliance, or in a superpower deterrent system. These models of world order have in common that they rely on an overwhelming central accumulation of force.

Such arguments are not to be lightly dismissed; people will not surrender their right to defence. The right to life and self-determination implies a right of defence. It will be quite impossible therefore to make any significant progress towards disarmament without at the same time developing alternative systems of defence; and if this cannot be based on military power, it must be based on something else.

We now have to question the doctrine that power comes out of the barrel of a gun. It is a doctrine

151

which is widely accepted because it is easy to understand. Threat and submission is a familiar form of social interaction, and this form of interaction can be seen as the basis of a certain form of social order, in which threats are passed down a pyramid of power. Some animal societies are constituted in this way; and any gangster who is prepared to wield a knife can soon create a miniature hierarchy of this kind, even in our own most 'civilised' society. The threat structure is part of the reality of political power — as Amin and Hitler demonstrated; but even in those extreme cases it was only a part, and the structure it produced was essentially transitory. The reality of power is more subtle.

Political power cannot exist in modern society without a highly complex system of compliance with laws and obedience to commands. People comply and obey for a variety of motives. Fear of violent sanctions is one motive, rarely operative in normal adult life; fear of social or economic consequences of non-compliance is another.

Of much greater importance however are the positive motivations which cause people to obey as a matter of habit. There is a sense of moral obligation, mixed with self-interest — an awareness that rules are needed, and that we are part of a whole system which only works because of habitual obedience. And, of course, there is 'pure habit', once perhaps based on other motivations, but long since totally self-sustaining — the way most people behave most of the time in complying with legal and social rules.

Political power not only depends on habitual obedience, it is actually *constituted* by habitual obedience. Without this obedience, there is no political power. It simply evaporates. Political power depends on the consent of the governed. Where an aggressive state 'takes over' another state and assumes political power, it must therefore take over an obedience system involving the entire population. If the governed
152

withdraw their consent, and oppose the take-over, political power evaporates. This has implications which are important for the future of world order.

There are many examples in history of power of oppressive regimes being opposed and neutralised by determined and co-ordinated opposition, sometimes quite unsupported by military force.

In 1920, a military coup in Germany was defeated in four days by a general strike. The self-appointed military dictators had no officials to carry out their commands — no typists even to type their letters, no postmen to deliver them, no means of transport, and no-one to supply them with their necessities. A military historian of the time sums up the episode simply by saying "To all intents and purposes the coup seemed to have succeeded; yet it was broken because the people would not obey the new government."*

In the 1930s, Gandhi organised in India a 'grand strategy' for obtaining a total British evacuation of India without firing a shot, much of his campaign being directed from prison. In 1942, during the occupation of Norway, the Nazis decided to use teachers to set up a fascist youth movement. The plan was backed with threats, torture, and the complete apparatus of Nazi prison camps for non-compliance. It was abandoned after 8 months and all imprisoned teachers were released.

These examples may seem insignificant in comparison with the problem of international defence; but they indicate an important line of progress. If so much can be achieved by spontaneous and unplanned opposition of limited numbers of people to oppressive rule, how much more could be achieved by highly planned and co-ordinated action of entire populations?

The examples quoted above are all of non-violent action. The lesson of liberation movements today is that violent action supported by large numbers can also succeed against overwhelming military odds. This

* Goodspeed, *The Comspirators*, pp. 211-13.

is the lesson of Vietnam and Afghanistan. What is more, deterrence can work with resistance movements just as much as with nuclear weapons. It is generally agreed that Yugoslavia survived for 30 years unmolested by the Soviet Union because Tito had organised the entire population in such a way that in the event of a Russian occupation it would split up into guerrilla bands in total opposition to the invaders. It is not surprising that the invaders did not arrive.

In the human rights perspective, alternative defence depends on making a reality of the principle that political power is based on the consent of the governed, and that people freely choose the political system within which they live. The more this principle is a reality upon which whole populations will act, the less does 'conquest' make any sense. Already in countries where this principle is fairly well-rooted, internal 'conquest' in the form of military 'coups' is unlikely; British prime ministers are safe from military coups — but not from the electorate. But the very beliefs and traditions which deprive internal conquest of meaning can also deprive external conquest of meaning, and gradually make the whole concept of military take-over 'mad' in the literal sense of the word.

Imaginative thinking about alternative defence and the basis of political power will eventually change the context of fear and anxiety which is one of the constraints on dismantling the existing system. Alternative defence thinking however depends on a heightened political awareness and heightened self-confidence; and the inspiration for that is coming from elsewhere.

SELF-DETERMINATION AND INTERNATIONAL ORDER

The power of national liberation movements could be a key to unlock some of the problems of international structure; but before we can use the key, it is important to understand how liberation movements actually affect the structure.

154

First of all, national liberation movements are part of the history of the principle of self-determination which is the foundation of human rights. Historically, it is impossible to separate the *principle* of self-determination from the *battle* for self-determination. The principle of self-determination first emerged in international rhetoric in the war aims of the Allies in the First World War — because it was obviously in their interests to support the forces of nationalism which were disrupting the empires of their enemies the Turks and Austrians; but the rhetoric only made political sense because it connected with real liberation movements.

We are now again in a situation where the right of self-determination can grow because it has become a force which is politically relevant. The stronger the national liberation movements on the 'ramparts' of the opposing empires, the less able are these empires to repair these ramparts by intervention. At a certain point, intervention becomes counter-productive in two senses. It becomes counter-productive in the military sense, because an increasing amount of military force has to be used to hold the people down, with a consequent weakening of the defence posture; and it is counter-productive ideologically, because intervention forces populations into the opposite ideological camp — just as the force of Vietnamese and Cuban nationalism was harnessed to communism by the Americans, and the force of Polish nationalism is being harnessed to anti-communism by the Russians.

The difficulties confronting the United States in Central America and Russia in Poland are similar in important respects.

In both cases, the logic of the bi-polar system suggests military intervention to maintain ramparts. However, there are also very strong forces acting on both sides against military intervention. The most powerful deterrent to such intervention is the resistance to be expected from the people whose territory is to be invaded. It is no secret that the Poles regard the Russians with hostility, just as Latin Americans (the people, not their ruling elites) regard the United States with hostility; and the basis of this hostility is the resistance that people normally show to domination by an alien power — whether that domination is due to the 'political imperialism' of Russia or the economic imperialism of the U.S.A.

This resistance to foreign domination is closely bound up with the internal battle for human rights. In Poland, the fight is for civil liberties, for free elections, for less censorship, for more real choice in the political system — for all those rights normally championed in the West and neglected in the East. In Guatemala and El Salvador the battle is for economic and social rights, against the grinding poverty and destitution of people deprived of land and basic resources, for all those rights championed in the East, and commonly neglected in the West. In 1974, 14 strikers in the Polish town of Gdansk were shot, thus preparing the way for the present much stronger civil rights movement. In 1978, more than 100 peasants meeting to protest over the land problem in the Guatemalan village of Panzós were mown down by machine gunners from the rooftops, adding fuel to the growing Indian revolutionary movement.

In Eastern Europe and Central America the opposing superpowers therefore face serious dilemmas. If they do not act, the ramparts of their empires will continue to crumble; if they do act, they will be seen throughout the world as the enemies of human rights, and the very foundations of their empires will be shaken by the reacting forces of liberation.

It is precisely in such dilemmas that initiatives which lay the foundations of a new kind of order are required, and that they have most chance of being adopted, since the failure of the existing system makes it necessary to look for a new one. The crisis area of the existing system should be regarded as the seedbeds of a new world order. What would be the elements of this new order?

The objective of the new order must be to maintain human rights more adequately than the present order. The human rights in question are the fundamental ones of security and self-determination.

Since it is the growing pressure of human rights movements, reinforced by international acceptance of the right of self-determination, which is making the condominium structure difficult to maintain, an alternative policy would be to adopt a vigorous policy based clearly on human rights, and self-determination under international guarantee. This policy would apply first of all to the regions of high tension on the military and ideological ramparts of the two empires. It would have both a negative and a positive aspect. On the negative side, there would have to be a strict regime of non-intervention by either side, except in ways totally acceptable to both sides and to the host country. On the positive side, there would have to be explicit and verifiable moves towards the realisation of human rights on a basis of self-determination.

Apart from these general principles there cannot be any rule of thumb solutions to be applied to all cases alike, because each case is different. In some cases big moves could be made, in others only small moves; but it is the direction which is important, rather than the distance covered.

Lord Carrington's proposal for the neutralisation of Afghanistan under international control is a move in the right direction. Poland, which is mainly Russia's problem does not present as yet the same possibilities because of the military significance of Poland to Russia's European defence position. The Polish civil rights movement is strong and healthy and the main objective of international diplomacy should be to strengthen it. In Central America, which is mainly America's problem, the scope is greater. These small republics are seething with a new found political awareness. They are not important for the USA in a military sense, but rather in an ideological and economic sense. America's dilemma is the world's opportunity.

A negative policy of non-intervention is not sufficient. There must also be bold and imaginative moves to express an international commitment to human rights in these countries, and therefore to the initiation of a world order radically different from that of the bipolar empire. Self-determination must mean sooner or later the holding of internationally supervised free elections. Revolutionaries in the heat of conflict tend understandably to push aside such thoughts; but the principle of self-determination as the basis of a new world order must have a defined and verifiable basis.

An outstanding achievement of the present British government was to initiate in Zimbabwe an internationally supervised election, resulting in the choice of a government which beyond all argument reflected the will of the majority of the people, though not the will of the British government itself.

This popular government in Zimbabwe immediately received international recognitition, and is a foundation stone of a new order in Southern Africa.

Afghanistan, Namibia, Eastern Europe, and Central America are regions of great danger in the world, but could also be the regions of great hope. Every country in which the principle of independence and self-determination is visibly established and from which Russian and American intervention is excluded, is a building block for a new international order The foundations of this order are being dug by national liberation movements; but the footings must be laid in the trenches by international action based on human rights.

INTERNATIONAL ORDER

We are still left with the difficulty of national governments promoting human rights. Human rights are by
158

definition universal; national governments are territorial. It is perfectly sensible that governments should operate locally — that they should promote human rights in a defined area. Local governments cannot take on the job of promoting human rights world-wide; and on the other hand, they cannot ignore human rights world-wide, because of the inconsistency this would involve.

The only way out of this dilemma is to bring into existence appropriate forms of world organisation, which have as their specific task the promotion of human rights world-wide. They would then set the general rules within which local governments would operate; they would ensure overall justice between different regions of the world; they would enforce minimum standards throughout the world; they would ensure that offenders against human rights met with appropriate international condemnation.

Some people like to imagine a single world government in the form of a super-super power, making world laws and having supreme coercive power to see that these laws are carried out. The original concept of the Security Council in the United Nations was rather like this. The idea was that if five 'giants' agreed they could enforce their will anywhere. As it happened, they did not agree. It is improbable now that mankind will form a unitary world government backed by a supreme force; and this may be a good thing.

The real task of building world government is going on all the time, and it has many different facets. It goes on wherever human rights are the subject of international debate, organisation or executive action. It is being formed for example through the experience of United Nations peace-keeping forces; through the work of the Food and Agriculture Organisation; through the growing international network of non-governmental organisations in the field of health, housing, and development; and through the World Health Organisation.

159

National Governments are not competent to promote human rights world wide; but for this very reason they must carry out the job of midwives to the new structures of world order. The work of embodying guarantees of human rights world wide in international institutions is a task that may well take a century to complete. Like the cathedral builders of the Middle Ages, we are surrounded by the trenches, the masonry, the scaffolding, and odds and ends of equipment that could be the beginnings of a great structure. Many cathedrals took more than a hundred years to build, but their architects had a plan and a vision.

Our vision must be of a world order based firmly on universal principles of human rights, because there is no way to peace except through justice.

Chapter Eleven
THE SHAPE OF GOVERNMENT

The argument of this book is that the essential purpose of Government is to maintain and promote human rights. In this concluding chapter I would like to consider briefly how a human rights government might best be organised.

OBJECTIVES AND METHOD

It is important to define the objectives of a system before deciding how it should be designed. On these grounds there is a case for enacting a Bill of Rights, which would define the objectives of government. This would involve a new Constitutional Settlement.*

The British on the whole are proud of their 'unwritten constitution', and some people will take the view that we have got on very well so far without a Bill of Rights, and by relying on a kind of pragmatic wisdom, 'feeling our way forward' and adapting to change as we always have done. There is a great deal to be said for this approach, and it has served us well in the past, but times are changing. The human rights movement is becoming a powerful national and international

* The argument for a Bill of Rights has been ably developed by Lord Scarman — *English Law — the New Dimension*, Hamlyn Lectures, published Stevens 1974 — to whom the reader is referred for exposition.

force, but it faces stormy waters. We are faced with inconsistencies between British Law and the international law of human rights. The pragmatic approach itself suggests that it is important now to chart a clear course, and that what was once implicit must now become explicit.

There are two aspects to the British human rights tradition; one is embodied in the Common Law, and the other in the political process.

The Common Law evolved over many centuries out of customary law developed by judges in relation to specific cases, and embodying basic principles of equality and fairness which command the consent and respect of the people. Because it developed independently of parliament or any other power centre, it became an effective bulwark against oppression and tyranny from any quarter. The political tradition has also moved, fairly steadily, in the direction of promoting fundamental human rights; it has secured universal suffrage, the right to participate in government; the right to education, and to a decent standard of living.

The 'statute laws' enacted by parliament were originally seen as supplements to common law; and the common law remained in theory the fundamental law of the land, able to stand up for the citizens' rights even against government. Parliament however as the enactor of new rules became increasingly the dominant partner in this joint enterprise, and during the nineteenth century it became generally accepted that Parliament had 'unrestricted sovereignty' i.e. it could make or unmake any laws it wished, including of course laws which revised or abolished aspects of the Common Law. Judges therefore could be obliged to enforce judgements they considered clearly contrary to long-established common law principles of human rights, if such was the express will of parliament expressed in statute law.

The rising tide of the human rights movement has

now placed the British Government in a difficult position. By ratifying the European Convention for the Protection of Human Rights and Fundamental Freedoms, the U.K. has recognised and declared the existence of rights which cannot be unmade by parliament.

Parliament itself therefore, in common with most governments of the world, has acknowledged a kind of 'common law of mankind' based not on the sovereignty of the state but on principles of natural justice. Yet neither the Declaration of 1948 nor the Convention of 1950 is part of the municipal law of the United Kingdom; they can only be made so by an Act of Parliament. Such an act is now called for on grounds of consistency alone. It would mean establishing human rights as a set of 'entrenched provisions' in the constitution.

That does not mean however that we should substitute judge-made law for parliament-made law, or that politics become a process of conforming to a set of preordained standards. It would be totally wrong to regard either the Courts or Parliament as the 'dominant' partner in this process of realising justice in society. They are practising two different and complementary forms of activity; both are equally concerned with justice and neither one makes sense without the other.

A Bill of Rights established and publicly proclaimed as the basic objective of Government, and including both Economic and Civil rights, would not just act as a 'brake' on government activity, providing a 'legal' remedy for this or that abuse of power; it would also provide a starting point and inspiration for all creative political programmes, a touchstone of their authenticity; and a measure for their success or failure.

The *methods* by which government should carry out its task of promoting human rights follow from the nature of these rights.

In broad terms, I have distinguished three kinds of

163

government activity — enabling, purchasing and providing. Since all human rights are rooted in freedom and self-determination, then the enabling function is always to be preferred. *Enabling* however does not just mean keeping out of the way. It means creating a framework of justice within which energies can be liberated. This means continuous vigilance against cancerous accumulations in a society of power or wealth without responsibility; and it means devising rules of the game which are clear and which involve the minimum of bureaucratic control.

Purchasing on behalf of the community is a second important method by which government can act. Some public purchasing of indivisible goods may be essential to maintain human rights; but often there is public purchasing of goods and services which people should be 'enabled' individually or communally to purchase for themselves.

Provision by government, a third method of activity, means that government actually delivers goods and services through its own machinery — as with the armed forces, the fire brigade or refuse disposal. Public provision may also be necessary in certain cases to maintain human rights; but provision is at the opposite extreme from enabling, and in view of its disabling implications it should be handled with extreme care.

SLIMMING THE SYSTEM

Having defined the objectives and methods of government, we should then be able to modify the existing system so that it is better able to fulfil those objectives. It is much too fat, and needs to slim — not so that it can achieve less, but so that it can achieve more, perhaps with less effort.

Much of the colossal growth of government which we described in the opening chapter has been well-motivated and vaguely related to human rights; but in general there has been confusion about objectives, and government has become like a well-meaning but half-blind dinosaur unable to perceive the damage it is doing, and with a brain too small to understand its own malfunctioning.

A good example of this growth has been in the field of industry, especially in the nationalisation programme of the 1940s. Nationalisation was based on the reasonable view that certain key industries which were vital to the well-being of society should be owned and controlled by the whole community through the national government, which would ensure that they were run for public benefit and not for private gain.

Behind this language however there was a good deal of mythology and a good deal of confusion. Industry is not just a system to generate private gain, it is also a system for delivery of goods and services which people need and will buy. What happens to this system when an industry is taken over by government in the name of the people? Does it then start to be concerned with people other that those who purchase its goods and services? If so, with which other people, and to what extent? Should it operate for profit and make as much money as possible for the government to spend on other things? Or should it provide goods and services for nothing to those who need them?

Incredible as it may seem, none of these questions was answered. A Report of a Select Committee on the Nationalised Industries in 1980 stated that a

165

'remarkable feature' of the nationalised industries was the extent to which vital issues like pricing policies or the relationship to government were left unclear; and that whereas the purpose of nationalisation had been that government would not interfere with management, but would provide general guidelines, what had happened was that government *did* interfere but did *not* provide guidelines!

Government does have a number of important jobs to do in relation to industry. It must for instance make rules governing safety standards both for workers and for consumers; work out taxation policies to allocate to industry an appropriate share of the cost of a social wage; enact and implement monopoly legislation to dissolve excessive agglomerations of power, and company legislation to provide a just and democratic framework for corporate activity. This enabling/rule-making activity applies to all industry, public or private. Problems of 'fat' arise with heavy Government involvement in the purchasing and providing roles, whether in the nationalised or semi-nationalised industries or as investor/supporter in a wide range of other industries, and it is in this field that difficulties will arise because of the involvement of government and industry, especially if industry has clear objectives and government only has vague ones. One danger is simply waste of public resources. The nuclear power programme and 'Concorde' are examples of how large amounts of public money can be committed to projects which private industry would not touch on commercial grounds, and for which there is no basis in human rights or trusteeship.

Health and Social Services represent another area of extraordinary growth in government activity closely linked (as in the case of housing) to a genuine concern for human rights. In this case also, the involvement of government has taken the form of large-scale centralised purchasing and provision of goods and services — hospitals, social workers, doctors, medical workers.

166

The dangers of the central 'providing' activity of government in the health and social service field are now easy to recognise, not only in this country but throughout the world. The providing model has generated in the people a corresponding 'dependency disease', and has deprived them of the element of self-determination and responsibility that we are now beginning to see is essential to the health of individuals and local communities. Ever increasing demand for health services and social services is met by ever decreasing ability of government to supply these services. The providing system moreover involves a large and complex bureaucracy to 'deliver' the goods and services required; and this large and complex bureaucracy develops its own purposes, not necessarily related to people's needs.

Experience has shown that this trend can be reversed.* The movement for self-help and care in the community is gathering strength. In Wiltshire, an adventurous Social Services Department has pioneered projects which are specifically designed to release the pent-up energy of the community. Voluntary day-care centres for the aged and disabled, operating in 20 villages with the help of a grant of £1,000 p.a. from the local authority, are providing support at a tenth of the cost of residential care, and with great benefit to the quality of village life. Publicly provided residential care for children, the disabled and the mentally ill is being systematically reduced, and the large sums of money thus released are being re-used to trigger off schemes of community self-help. Private and voluntary organisations are being encouraged to accept more responsibility. No day nurseries are provided for the under fives; but the County has the most developed Pre-School Playgroup organisation in the

* Alternative Ways of Providing Social Services, Don Latham (Assistant Director of Social Services, Wiltshire County Council) Article in *Public Money*, 1981.

country, and because of the number of family centres which have been developed, in co-operation with private and voluntary organisations, there is now a wide range of facilities for young children at a cost far below the national average.

Even in the field of internal security, it should not be too easily assumed that 'providing' is the only option open to government. Alternative policing systems develop spontaneously when existing systems fail. A Marxist Worker Defence Group protects immigrants against racial persecution in London. Householders unable to obtain protection against burglars form mutual protection clubs. In the United States, local communities take joint action against muggers, by carrying whistles and agreeing that all householders will instantly turn out on the street when a whistle is heard. New Jersey has its own private police force; and perhaps most interesting of all, Disneyland in the United States with an ever changing population the size of a small city has almost no crime due to a straightforward 'best buy' public purchasing approach to crime prevention on the part of the Disneyland authorities.

There is now a wealth of experiment into methods of 'enabling' which reduces the cost and bureaucracy of government, and which offer a very satisfactory 'slimming guide' for governments determined to promote human rights and freedoms.

CHOOSING A GOVERNMENT

The next question to ask is what is the best way to choose a government — i.e. what is the best way to choose a committee to promote human rights in a particular territory?

It is important to tackle this question in the same down-to-earth way that we would tackle any other question of choosing a group of people to do a specific job. Because of the confusion of politics with mythology, however, there are some myths that have to be
168

dispersed before the question can be tackled. These myths are dogmatic and often cherished beliefs which express important truths in a symbolic form, but which can be obstacles to solving problems unless the mythology is properly interpreted.

Myths

The first myth is the belief that government represents the people. A representative, in ordinary usage, is a person who stands in for someone else — when you speak to him, it is as if you were speaking to the represented person, and when he speaks, he speaks fo for the represented person. This arrangement is a very useful one in everyday life, but the situation in which representation functions has to be closely defined, and the subject matter of the representation also has to be defined, in a kind of 'contract of representation'. Thus a lawyer can represent you in a legal dispute, or a colleague at a committee meeting.

The larger the group of people who are 'represented', and the wider the situation and range of subjects about which they are represented, the more difficult this contact becomes. If you were representing two people simultaneously, you would either have to make two different 'representations', or assume the people you were representing both had identical views. This might be possible if the subject matter was specific and limited — like representing in a planning appeal a village which wants (or does not want) a motorway. If however the number of people represented is large, and the subject matter broad and ill-defined, the task of a representative is virtually impossible.

Parliamentary 'representation' is at the extreme point of this spectrum of possibilities. In this case, many thousands of people every five years are asked to cast a vote to select one of two or three people to 'represent' them about a vast range of issues, many of which do not even exist at the time of voting, and

169

most of which are very little understood either by voters or representatives. Of course, there remain occasional specific issues where someone in a constituency can 'nobble' his M.P. and get some action, but these situations, though important, are the exception in the life of an M.P., and most of the time the idea of 'representing' so many thousands of people in the national rule-making process is a pure 'myth' — not because of any human fault, but simply because the word 'represent' as we normally use it does not fit the situation. If we continue to use the word 'represent' for the M.P.'s function — as we certain will — then it needs a separate paragraph in the New English Dictionary.

The second myth that needs dispersing before asking the question about how to choose a government is embodied in the statement that 'the majority is always right'. It requires only a moment's reflection to appreciate the mythological nature of this statement. When we are faced with a problem, we do not normally decide which is the correct answer by taking a majority vote. The majority is often wrong about many things, but specifically is is often wrong about human rights — sometimes hideously wrong. A popular sport in ancient Rome, supported by a large majority, was to feed Christians to the lions — a practice which we believe today to be contrary to human rights. To bring the point closer to home, many people would hold that the Protestant majority in Northern Ireland has been for many years seriously mistaken about the human rights of the Catholic minority, with disastrous consequences for the social order.

The third myth is connected with the other two, and is more subtle. This is the belief that government (identified with the nation-state) should be in some way a 'self-realisation' of the people, so that in some mystical sense it 'is' the people. This gets rid of the problem of representation, because if the state embodied in the government 'is' the people, the people are there in person and do not even have to be represented. It also avoids the problem of the majority often being wrong, because if a majority government 'is' the people then there is nothing left to say the government is wrong except non-people.

Universal Suffrage

Let us return now to consider the down-to-earth question of how best to choose a government. First of all, who should do the choosing?

The best group of people to choose a committee responsible for human rights in a particular territory is an association of all the people who live in that territory, all having an 'equal say'. The reason for this is simple. The best group of people to select any committee is the people concerned with the job the committee is doing. If it is the darts committee, then the darts players should choose it. If it is the human rights committee, then all the people should choose it, because they are all equally concerned with human rights, and they are all equal in dignity and rights. Moreover, since rights are based on fundamental needs, we would expect everyone to be competent to do this job, because people know when their fundamental needs are not being met.

If candidates for government office seek election by the people, they should (and usually do) claim that they will maintain and promote human rights, and meet fundamental human needs; and on this basis they will be chosen. If they fail, the people are likely to know they have failed because they will be aware that their basic rights have not been met. Everyone can be expected to know, if their attention is directed to those issues, whether they and their friends have satisfying work, a home, security, civil rights, educational opportunities, a healthy environment, and adequate food, or whether progress is being made in these fields, and if it is clear to them that the basic

171

function of government is to achieve those objectives, they will be able to assess the government's success.

People therefore are competent or potentially competent to act in the selection process just because they are human; and it is also essential that *all* the human beings are included in this electoral function, because the objective is to maintain *human* rights — not the rights of any particular class, creed, race or age group. Perception can play strange tricks. In a television interview shortly after the election of the first prime minister of Zimbabwe, a white woman said, in all seriousness to the interviewer, against the background of roaring and jubilant crowds thronging the streets, '*Nobody* wants Mugabe.' Her concept of what constitutes a human being was obviously limited.

It might be objected that if people only vote on the grounds of whether fundamental rights are met they will usually be thinking in the short-term. They might not make wise calculations about whether a government's policies are leading towards a better society in the future.

It is true that a person who is homeless and out of work is not likely to vote for a government which he sees as the cause of his deprivation or which is preoccupied with other matters; he will not be easily persuaded to vote for this government by long-term consideration of public benefit. But this may be no bad thing. There is something absolute about rights. The concept of rights implies that people cannot be treated as a means to an end.

Parties

Assuming that it is up to an association of all the people to choose the government, who should they choose from? Evidently there must be some alternatives to choose from, otherwise there is no choice; and there must be some means of rejecting an unsatisfactory government without entering into the chaos of non-government.

172

This is the basic logic behind the party system in politics. In order that the people may have some kind of choice, it is essential to agglomerate the many possible approaches to government into 'bundles' of people and opinions, and to offer these bundles as it were 'for sale'. Schumpeter defined democracy as 'an institutional arrangement for arriving at political decisions in which individuals acquire power to decide by means of a competitive struggle for the people's vote.'

There is nothing here to set the imagination on fire, or to summon the masses to the barricades. But there is nevertheless something very important about the combination of universal suffrage and a freely generated party system which revolutionaries must not neglect. Self-determination of peoples, as we have seen, is a fundamental and pervasive principle of the international law. Article 1 of the International Human Rights Covenant affirms that:

> All people have the right of self-determination. By virtue of that right they freely determine their political status and freely pursue their economic, social and cultural development.

Also guaranteed is the right to universal suffrage and free expression of the will of electors.*

It is difficult to see how any content can be given to these fundamental rights, or how people can 'choose' their government in any meaningful sense, unless there is something like a multi-party system and a real possibility of refusing assent to a bad administration. It may well be that many 'one party' states rule with the consent of the people; but we have no means of knowing this, and neither have the governments concerned.

The 'market' image of the political party system may seem crude to the idealist; but it is real. And the difference between politicians having to pay attention

---

* See Article 25 of the International Covenant on Civil and Political Rights.

to the people in a multi-party system and having to pay attention to the party machine in a one party system is different not just of degree but of kind.

It is essential however to keep the party system in perspective. It is a device to give meaning to the people's right 'freely to choose' their government; and government itself is a system for promoting human rights. Parties themselves don't have rights; only people have rights. If parties function in a way that deprives people of the right 'freely to choose', or in a way that undermines human rights, then they lose the reason for their existence.

Voting and the party system are neither more nor less than useful practical devices for choosing a government, avoiding dictatorship, and promoting human rights. They are neither mystical nor infallible. Nothing is more dangerous to democracy than the pursuit of 'perfect democracy' — the machine-state, in which perfect parties perfectly represent the people. Human communities are not at all like machines, made out of cog-wheels mechanically interacting. They are social organisms, bound together by trust and respect. If political systems are designed like machines, they will either be bad machines, or, more likely, they will be taken over by dictators who like to manipulate human machines — and that is how human rights are destroyed.

Proportional Representation

Given that every person should have an 'equal say' in choosing the government, can we say anything further about how that 'equal say' should be organised, about the actual *voting system* — apart from the obvious need for freedom and fairness?

A simple one man one vote system, and a simple majority election in each district such as we have in Britain is in general unsatisfactory. The reason for this is that it tends to favour a 'majority tyranny', especially where there are deep divisions of interest
174

and opinion within the society in question.

It is easy to see why this is so. If 55% of the people vote for party A, and 45% for party B, and these people are evenly spread through the territory, then party A will always form the government and no members of party B will ever be elected. This means that the government will tend to concern itself with the rights of the A voters, and not the rights of the B voters, i.e. they will not be concerned with human rights but with the rights of certain groups. The A government will be reinforced by the myth that the majority is always right, or that it has a right to do whatever it chooses; whereas in reality the government only has a 'right' to do its job — i.e. to promote human rights. Majority voting is no more than a way of choosing people to do that job.

On the other hand, where there are two conflicting groups in a territory which do have both a chance of 'winning', the simple majority system tends to confirm and deepen the divisions within society and to generate the style of election called 'adversary politics'. This is the peculiarly British disease of the past 35 years, when each of two major parties claim a monopoly of wisdom, and comes 'into power' to undo the work of its predecessor. This is a cause of disorder and uncertainty in society, and obstructs long-term planning. It is also hugely wasteful of resources.

The two party mould based on a simple majority vote is difficult to break because no new group can gain any power through the system until it has gained nearly a third of the votes.

In general the simple majority is suspect as a basis for selecting a human rights government, because of the danger of sectional tyranny. The danger is compounded within such an electoral system if any particular power-group (such as the trade unions), is given a weighted position in elections, not based on the free votes of individual human beings. Such a practice is directly contrary to international human

175

rights conventions, and is not an appropriate method to choose a government.

A better system is a form of what is known as 'proportional representation', now well established and tested in European countries. Of all existing systems the Irish Single Transferable Vote seems best. In this system voters are asked to list a number of candidates in order of preference, second and subsequent preferences being taken into account in order to select M.P.s according to popularity ranking. This helps smaller parties to emerge and ensures that any substantial minority groups are able to choose people who will 'stand for' their rights. This means in turn that the government tends to be formed of coalitions, and is less able to exercise the tyranny of the majority, or to fall under the domination of any power group, since it must keep an eye on a wider section of the total population whose rights it exists to promote. Throughout the recent history of Northern Ireland, proportional representation tended to reduce the influence of military factions, whereas straight majority voting favoured extremism on both sides.

It is however important to remember that what we have been discussing in this section is how to choose a government which will be responsible for promoting human rights. If there is no such agreement about the basic function of government, then clearly there can be no agreement about how to choose it. If a government is chosen for something other than human rights, such as promoting economic growth or building an empire, it would have to be chosen in a different way. If on the other hand government is a committee 'for everything', and has no agreed function, then there will certainly never be agreement about how to choose its members. The same argument applies to other important structural aspects of government — the separation of powers in the executive, the judiciary, and the legislature; the second House; the cabinet system, and the role of the Civil Service.

176

Agreement about all these presupposes agreement about what government is for. It is impossible to plan a route without first agreeing about the destination.

THE DANGER AND THE HOPE

Totalitarianism, in any one of its many forms, is the main threat we have to face in the latter part of the twentieth century.

One reason for this is the development of large centralised technologies on which we are increasingly dependent. If a society depends for its existence on a system that can easily be controlled by a few people, then clearly there is a technological basis for totalitarianism which does not exist where there is no such structure.

One of the longest lived of human tyrannies was that of ancient Egypt; and this Egyptian tyranny had as its basis the complicated and centrally controlled system of irrigation canals which literally brought life to the desert, and on which the whole civilisation was totally dependent. This system was controlled by the central bureaucracy.

No one would want to compare the Central Electricity Generating Board with the Pharaohs of ancient Egypt. Yet the two are not unconnected, and the generation of nuclear power with its attendant risks could involve a considerable extension of the police power.

A second cause of danger today is social unrest. A quarter of the countries in the world are in a state of near revolution or internal warfare. Within the United Kingdom, racial tensions are now beginning to surface in riots, sometimes aimed specifically at the police. Violence and disorder in society is generally associated with a denial of human rights. Human beings, en masse, are not gratuitously violent, though some sick individuals may be. They are violent when their fundamental needs as human beings are systematically obstructed, and they can find no alternative means of

177

expression or self-realisation. Violence and disorder is the principle breeding ground for dictatorship. It is exceedingly difficult to prevent violence breeding violence; and this sets into operation a chain reaction which leads to a dictatorship of violence as the only means of preserving 'order'. Society then becomes a pyramid legitimised only by force, and is no longer based on the consent of the governed.

The third cause of danger is ideological; and this is the greatest danger of all, because the ideas can appeal to the noblest part of a man and yet lead to his destruction. A particular danger likes in those rational arguments which tend to exalt the power and authority of the democratic state.

One argument is based on accountability. Only the government, it is argued, is truly 'accountable' to the people, because it is the only complete 'accountability machine'. The people choose the government, and the government represents the people, to whom it is accountable. In theory, there exists a perfect system of accountability based on the sovereignty of the people.

The reality of accountability as we know is quite different, because people are not at all like machines. If they are treated like bits of machines, they will be bad machines — there will be slippage at every interface. The more links in the accountability chain, the less well it will function. Accountability through the immensely long chain of central government has many points of slippage. Not only are government servants not like cog wheels, the government bureaucracy as a whole is not like a machine either; it is a human association with its own life, its own hierarchy and purposes — its principle purpose, as in any human group, being to survive.

Treating government as the perfect 'accountability machine' results in practice in sucking more and more resources in to a central body which retains many resources for its own purposes, and disburses the rest

178

in a way which the general public can neither control nor comprehend.

Closely allied to the accountability argument is the argument that government is 'ultimately responsible' for whatever happens in society, or that its task is to avoid risk — arguments again based on a machine model of how human society coheres, a machine being necessarily complete and totally predictable.

Recognising these defects, the logical democrat may well try to remedy them by trying to improve the machine by adding further controls. He may favour more direct delegation, or participation of all in every level of government. In so doing he may mistake the *equal right to participate in government* with the *right to participate equally* in government — forgetting that the latter only existed in an ephemeral and unstisfactory way in the village-sized community of ancient Athens and even there it depended on slaves working in silver mines and farmsteads. Excessive participation of all in government is yet another royal road through disorder to dictatorship.

Underlying all these dangers which threaten freedom is a deeper danger related to more fundamental human behaviour patterns; that is the danger of idolatory.

It is characteristic of large and complex human societies to 'collapse inwards' about a central focus, and to abandon responsibility and judgement to a pivotal figure (human or otherwise), which is considered to embody some kind of divinity. It is as if we have not yet learned as a race how to cohere in large and complex groups without running the risk of inward collapse which produced the fossilised tyrannies associated with ancient Egypt, or with the last phase Maya civilisation, or with the late history of the Ashanti in North Africa. Often in the early history of these centripetal cultures we catch glimpses of an antecendent primitive culture which was much less centripetal, much more flexible, much more 'democratic according to our ways of thinking.

179

The human behaviour pattern which caused this sequence of events is still with us.

The Spanish philosopher Ortega y Gasset, wrote of the threatened absorption of all spontaneous social effort by the state, which is believed in the long run to sustain, nourish, and impel human destinies.

> When the mass suffers any ill-fortune or simply feels some strong appetite, its great temptation is that permanent, sure possibility of obtaining everything — without effort, struggle, doubt, or risk — merely by touching a button and setting the mighty machine in motion. The mass says to itself, 'L'Etat, c'est moi', which is a complete mistake. But the mass-man does in fact believe that he is the State, and he will tend more and more to set its machinery working on whatsoever pretext, to crush beneath it any creative minority which disturbs it — disturbs it in any order of things: in politics, in ideas, in industry.
>
> The result of this tendency will be fatal. Spontaneous social action will be broken up over and over again by State intervention; no new seed will be able to fructify. Society will have to live for the State, man for the governmental machine. And as, after all, it is only a machine whose existence and maintenance depend on the vital supports around it, the State, after sucking out the very marrow of society, will be left bloodless, a skeleton, dead with that rusty death of machinery, more gruesome than the death of a living organism.

It is not just the state, but individuals linked to it who are idolised. In a situation of chaos certain kinds of individual can acquire hypnotic power, a power related to certain charismatic capabilities, and not in any way to their competence, to solve the problem with which the people are confronted. The lesson of Adolf Hitler is one which every human society must internalise.

There is one antidote to all these dangers which threaten mankind as we move forward into the twenty first century. That antidote is a powerful, informed, and internationally articulated human informed and internationally articulated human rights movement, which will progressively unite the world in a brotherhood based on equality or respect, and gradually transform governments by defining them as the servants of the people.

The greatest source of hope for the future of mankind at the present time is in the rising tide of consciousness throughout the world that the battle for human rights is the real battle we all have to fight. Like all powerful movements in human history, the human rights movement is nourished by the blood of martyrs. In 1980 Archbishop Romero of El Salvador, (the 'land of the Redeemer') was shot as he celebrated mass. He was one of the greatest and most courageous spokesmen for human rights in the world, and his death epitomises the deaths of many thousands who have suffered as victims of oppression in Poland, Nazi Germany, Russia, Ireland, Cambodia, Vietnam, Honduras, Uganda, and many other countries where tyranny has raged for a while apparently unchecked.

It is for all of us in our everyday lives and our politics to make sense of their sacrifice.

Appendix
THE UNIVERSAL DECLARATION
OF HUMAN RIGHTS

The following Declaration was adopted by the General Assembly of the United Nations in December 1948.

The Declaration is not legally binding as such. It is however an authoritative guide to the interpretation of the U.N. Charter, and is regarded by the Assembly and by some jurists as part of the 'law of the United Nations'.

The Declaration has formed the basis of international covenants which are binding, notably the International Covenant on Economic Social and Cultural Rights and the International Covenant on Civil and Political Rights, both of which entered into force in 1976 with over 60 states having become parties to them.

The Helsinki Declaration of 1975, signed by representatives of 35 States (including the USA and the USSR), included a passage reaffirming the Universal Declaration of Human Rights.

Preamble

Whereas recognition of the inherent dignity and of the equal and inalienable rights of all members of the human family is the foundation of freedom, justice and peace in the world,

Whereas disregard and contempt for human rights have resulted in barbarous acts which have outraged the conscience of mankind, and the advent of a world in which human beings shall enjoy freedom of speech and belief and freedom from fear and want has been proclaimed as the highest aspiration of the common people,

Whereas it is essential, if man is not to be compelled to have recourse, as a last resort, to rebellion against tyranny and oppression, that human rights should be protected by the rule of law,

Whereas it is essential to promote the development of friendly relations between nations,

Whereas the people of the United Nations have in the Charter reaffirmed their faith in fundamental human rights, in the dignity and worth of the human person and in the equal rights of men and women and have determined to promote social progress and better standards of life in large freedom,

Whereas Member States have pledged themselves to achieve, in co-operation with the United Nations, the promotion of universal respect for and observance of human rights and fundamental freedoms,

Whereas a common understanding of these rights and freedoms is of the greatest importance for the full realization of this pledge.

Now, Therefore,

The General Assembly

proclaims

This universal declaration of human rights as a common standard of achievement for all peoples and all nations, to the end that every individual and every organ of society, keeping this Declaration constantly in mind, shall strive by teaching and education to promote respect for these rights and freedoms and by progressive measures, national and international, to secure their universal and effective recognition and observance, both among the peoples of Member States themselves and among the peoples of territories under their jurisdiction.

Article 1

All human beings are born free and equal in dignity and rights. They are endowed with reason and conscience and should act towards one another in a spirit of brotherhood.

Article 2

Everyone is entitled to all the rights and freedoms set forth in this Declaration, without distinction of any kind, such as race, colour, sex, language, religion, political or other opinion, national or social origin, property, birth or other status.

Furthermore, no distinction shall be made on the basis of the political, jurisdictional or international status of the country or territory to which a person belongs, whether it be independent, trust, non-self-governing or under any other limitations of sovereignty.

Article 3

Everyone has the right to life, liberty and security of person.

Article 4

No one shall be held in slavery or servitude; slavery and the slave trade shall be prohibited in all their forms.

Article 5

No one shall be subjected to torture or to cruel, inhuman or degrading treatment or punishment.

Article 6

Everyone has the right to recognition everywhere as a person before the law.

Article 7

All are equal before the law and are entitled without any discrimination to equal protection of the law. All are entitled to equal protection against any discrimination in violation of this Declaration and against any incitement to such discrimination.

Article 8

Everyone has the right to an effective remedy by the competent national tribunals for acts violating the fundamental rights granted him by the constitution or by law.

Article 9

No one shall be subjected to arbitrary arrest, detention or exile.

Article 10

Everyone is entitled in full equality to a fair and public hearing by an independent and impartial tribunal, in the determination of his rights and obligations and of any criminal charge against him.

Article 11

1. Everyone charged with a penal offence has the right to be presumed innocent until proved guilty according to law in a public trial at which he has had all the guarantees necessary for his defence.
2. No one shall be held guilty of any penal offence on account of any act or omission which did not constitute a penal offence, under national or international law, at the time when it was committed. Nor shall a heavier penalty be imposed than the one that was applicable at the time the penal offence was committed.

Article 12

No one shall be subjected to arbitrary interference with his privacy, family, home or correspondence, nor to attacks upon his honour and reputation. Everyone has the right to the protection of the law against such interference or attacks.

Article 13

1. Everyone has the right to freedom of movement and residence within the borders of each state.
2. Everyone has the right to leave any country, including his own, and to return to his country.

Article 14

1. Everyone has the right to seek and to enjoy in other countries asylum from persecution.
2. This right may not be invoked in the case of prosecutions genuinely arising from non-political crimes or from acts contrary to the purposes and principles of the United Nations.

Article 15

1. Everyone has the right to a nationality.
2. No one shall be arbitrarily deprived of his nationality nor denied the right to change his nationality.

Article 16

1. Men and women of full age, without any limitation due to race, nationality or religion, have the right to marry and to found a family. They are entitled to equal rights as to marriage, during marriage and at its dissolution.
2. Marriage shall be entered into only with the free and full consent of the intending spouses.
3. The family is the natural and fundamental group unit of society and is entitled to protection by society and the State.

Article 17

1. Everyone has the right to own property alone as well as in association with others.
2. No one shall be arbitrarily deprived of his property.

Article 18

Everyone has the right to freedom of thought, conscience and religion; this right includes freedom to change his religion or belief, and freedom, either alone or in community with others and in public or private, to manifest his religion or belief in teaching, practice, worship and observance.

Article 19

Everyone has the right to freedom of opinion and expression; this right includes freedom to hold opinions without interference and to seek, receive and impart information and ideas through any media and regardless of frontiers.

Article 20

1. Everyone has the right to freedom of peaceful assembly and association.
2. No one may be compelled to belong to an association.

Article 21

1. Everyone has the right to take part in the government of his country, directly or through freely chosen representatives.
2. Everyone has the right of equal access to public service in his country.
3. The will of the people shall be the basis of the authority of government; this will shall be expressed in periodic and genuine elections which shall be by universal and equal suffrage and shall be held by secret vote or by equivalent free voting procedures.

Article 22

Everyone, as a member of society, has the right to social security and is entitled to realization, through national effort and international co-operation and in accordance with the organization and resources of each State, of the economic, social and cultural rights indispensable for his dignity and the free development of his personality.

Article 23

1. Everyone has the right to work, to free choice of employment, to just and favourable conditions of work and to protection against unemployment.
2. Everyone, without any discrimination, has the right to equal pay for equal work.
3. Everyone who works has the right to just and favourable remuneration ensuring for himself and his familyan existence worthy of human dignity, and supplemented, if necessary, by other means of social protection.
4. Everyone has the right to form and join trade unions for the protection of his interests.

Article 24

Everyone has the right to rest and leisure, including reasonable limitation of working hours and periodic holidays with pay.

186

Article 25

1. Everyone has the right to a standard of living adequate for the health and well-being of himself and of his family, including food, clothing, housing and medical care and necessary social services, and the right to security in the event of unemployment, sickness, disability, widowhood, old age or other lack of livelihood in circumstances beyond his control.

2. Motherhood and childhood are entitled to special care and assistance. All children, whether born in or out of wedlock, shall enjoy the same social protection.

Article 26

1. Everyone has the right to education. Education shall be free, at least in the elementary and fundamental stages. Elementary education shall be compulsory. Technical and professional education shall be made generally available and higher education shall be equally accessible to all on the basis of merit.

2. Education shall be directed to the full development of the human personality and to the strengthening of respect for human rights and fundamental freedoms. It shall promote understanding, tolerance and friendship among all nations, racial or religious groups, and shall further the activities of the United Nations for the maintenance of peace.

3. Parents have a prior right to choose the kind of education that shall be given to their children.

Article 27

1. Everyone has the right freely to participate in the cultural life of the community, to enjoy the arts and to share in scientific advancement and its benefits.

2. Everyone has the right to the protection of the moral and material interests resulting from any scientific, litery or artistic production of which he is the author.

Article 28

Everyone is entitled to a social and international order in which the rights and freedoms set forth in this Declaration can be fully realized.

Article 29

1. Everyone has duties to the community in which alone the free and full development of his personality is possible.

2. In the exercise of his rights and freedoms, everyone shall be subject only to such limitations as are determined by law

solely for the purpose of securing due recognition and respect for the rights and freedoms of others and of meeting the just requirements of morality, public order and the general welfare in a democratic society.

3. These rights and freedoms may in no case be exercised contrary to the purposes and principles of the United Nations.

Article 30

Nothing in this Declaration may be interpreted as implying for any State, group or person any right to engage in any activity or to perform any act aimed at the destruction of any of the rights and freedoms set forth herein.

LOCAL INITIATIVES IN
GREAT BRITAIN

There is a lot of talk today about 'de-centralization', but this does not make any sense unless there are local groups able to accept the responsibilities handed over from the centre.

In the last few years there has been an extraordinary growth of local initiatives in forms such as

> Community Co-operatives
> Local Enterprise Trusts
> Town Development Trusts

Local Initiatives in Great Britain is a thoroughly researched set of profiles of all significant initiatives of this kind in the country. It is a basic reference book for all those who wish to understand or join in the movement.

The Foundation for Alternatives
The Rookery
Adderbury
Banbury
Oxon.

A5 - 126 pp - paperback
ISBN 0 9505081 9 5

also by STAN WINDASS

MAN DIVIDED

All men and women experience divisions
within themselves — of one kind or another.
Through the ages 'myths' have been used to
formulate or resolve the tensions resulting
from the experience.
This book draws widely on the literature of the
War between Good and Evil, Darkness and Light.
It shows how primitive myth patterns still govern
our thinking on politics, education, psychology,
and many other fields.
A provocative 'think' book, simply written,
which could well be used in schools.

available from

NEW FOUNDATIONS
THE ROOKERY
ADDERBURY
BANBURY
OX17 3NA

Cr. 8vo 104 pp paperback
SBN 232 51080 6

also by STAN WINDASS

POWER, POLITICS AND IDEALS

(Selected papers 1966-1970)

Historically it is impossible to separate the development of justice from the assertion of rights, sometimes through armed conflict. These papers examine a number of situations of international conflict, such as the Cuban missile crisis, the Indonesian struggle for independence, the disputes over the funding of UN peace-keeping activities, and a number of boundary disputes involving the League of Nations.

Originally published in the journal of the David Davies Memorial Institute of International Relations and in THE INTERNATIONAL REGULATION of FRONTIER DISPUTES (ed. Evan Luard; Thames & Hudson, 1970). Now available in one volume from

NEW FOUNDATIONS
THE ROOKERY
ADDERBURY
BANBURY
OX17 3NA

Cr. 8vo 120 pp
paperback